A DAY OF HISTORY

Pope Paul VI's unprecedented peace pilgrimage to the United States has transfixed the imagination of all peoples everywhere. This book is the permanent record of that unique and inspiring day of history. Here are the Pope's own words, which aroused the conscience of mankind. Here are the pictures of the spiritual leader who brought hope and faith to a troubled age. Here is the day as it actually took place, brought to life with an astonishing immediacy and intimacy by some of the leading journalists and photographers of our time.

THE POPE'S JOURNEY TO THE UNITED STATES

A BOOK FOR MEN AND WOMEN OF ALL FAITHS

A BOOK TO REMEMBER AND CHERISH FOREVER

Other members of the staff of
The New York Times
who participated in this project were:
Editors and reporters—
Sheldon J. Binn, Marshall E. Newton,
Kalman A. Seigel, Charlotte Curtis, William P. Luce,
Bob G. Slosser, Genell Subak-Sharpe and Robert Alden.
Editorial assistants—
Patrick R. Wallace, Carter B. Horsley, Harry V. Poloshjian,
Gilbert M. Haggerty and Stephen J. Moran.

THE POPE'S JOURNEY TO THE UNITED STATES

WRITTEN BY
STAFF MEMBERS OF *THE NEW YORK TIMES*
EDITED BY
A. M. ROSENTHAL AND ARTHUR GELB

ILLUSTRATED WITH PHOTOGRAPHS

B
P

THE POPE'S JOURNEY TO THE UNITED STATES
A Bantam Book / Published October 1965

Library of Congress Catalog Card Number: 65-28642
All rights reserved.
Copyright © 1965 by Bantam Books, Inc.

This book may not be reproduced in whole or in part, by mimeograph or any other means, without permission in writing.

Published simultaneously in the United States and Canada.

Bantam Books are published by Bantam Books, Inc., a subsidiary of Grosset & Dunlap, Inc. Its trade-mark, consisting of the words "Bantam Books" and the portrayal of a bantam, is registered in the United States Patent Office and in other countries. Marca Registrada. Bantam Books, Inc., 271 Madison Avenue, New York, N. Y. 10016.

Contents

Introduction

October 4, 1965, was a day of history and what happened that day and what was said by the visitor to the United Nations have become one of those particular moments that enter into the lives and memories of scores of millions of people.

For members of the staff of *The New York Times* it was a poignant day, perhaps the saddest professional day of our lives. The visit of the Pope was one of the best single stories in New York's history; nobody could remember many bigger ones. But it was the nineteenth day of a strike against *The Times* and our paper was not to be on the stands that day or the next morning. Every day, hour by hour, reporters and editors who were on strike and those of us who were not had been united by a deep, deep hope that the dispute would end in time for us to cover the Pope's visit, but it did not come about.

If *The Times* had published, Bantam Books would have reprinted in book form all our stories. This book is what *The Times* would have printed that day.

Several days before the visit Assistant Metropolitan Editor Arthur Gelb and I worked out the assignment sheet we would follow were we to print. When it seemed that we would not, the reporters who would have covered stories that day were asked if they would do the same stories for Bantam, to be edited by *Times* editors, also working that day for Bantam. The response was immediate, warm, professional.

On that day, the reporters went out into the streets of New York, covered the stories as if *The Times* had been publishing and then we all met to turn out this book in an impromptu newsroom at Bantam. We all would have been so much happier if we had been working in our own 229 West 43d Street. But we all have a feeling of satisfaction that on that moment in history we were able to do what we live to do—cover a story.

A. M. Rosenthal
Metropolitan Editor, *The New York Times*

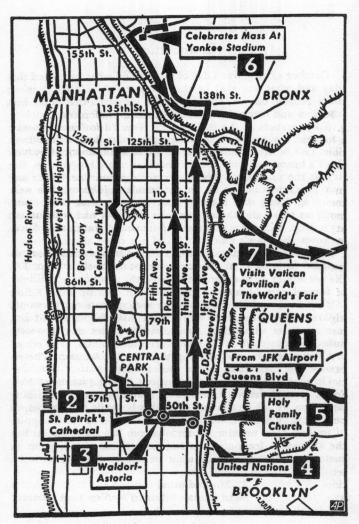

Itinerary of the Pope's visit.

An Historic Mission

By Homer Bigart

Pope Paul VI journeyed to the United Nations on October 4, 1965, to appeal to the leaders of the world for peace. It was a historic mission that transfixed a great city, seized the attention of millions of Americans throughout the country, of people around the globe.

The Pope's address was the focus of a fourteen-hour tour in which he also conferred with President Johnson, was welcomed by huge but orderly crowds on a twenty-four mile motorcade through the city, celebrated mass for ninety thousand at Yankee Stadium and visited the floodlit Vatican Pavilion at the World's Fair.

His mission of diplomacy marked the first visit of a reigning pontiff to the New World. It was an occasion that suspended the normal life of the city and affected the emotions of millions of persons of all faiths.

The Pope himself, often depicted as a man not given to high emotion, surprised the General Assembly by the vehemence of his appeal for peace in the name of war-weary humanity.

At one time his voice rose almost to a shout as he sternly exhorted the Assembly to end the threat of nuclear annihilation. Speaking in French, he cried: *"Jamais plus la guerre! Jamais plus la guerre!"* (No more war! No more war!) "It is peace, peace," he implored, "that should guide the destiny of peoples and all mankind."

This was the first time that a pontiff had appeared before the United Nations, and the challenge of Pope Paul VI, spiritual leader of half a billion Roman Catholics, to the chief secular organization of mankind was watched with rapt attention by world diplomats and guests within the high-ceilinged assembly chamber and by a television audience numbering hundreds of millions.

Pope Paul VI went to the United Nations after conferring with President Johnson at the Waldorf Towers. The escalation of the war in Vietnam, the American intervention in the Dominican Republic and the India-Pakistan fighting were among the subjects "discussed in some detail," President Johnson told reporters later.

The Pope said through an interpreter that he was very happy that the session with President Johnson "revolved about a mutual desire to work for peace."

The President escorted the Pope to the street, standing at the curb and waving as the Pontiff's motorcade returned to Cardinal Spellman's residence. This was a taut moment for the police. It was the only moment when the Pope and the President were exposed together to crowds.

For despite the tightest security precautions ever taken in New York, the Pope's visit was a nerve-racking test for the police and the Secret Service. It was feared that the Waldorf meeting might attract to the area not only dangerous political fanatics but also an entirely different type of extremist—the unbalanced religious zealot.

Police marksmen with rifles were stationed on strategic rooftops near the Waldorf. All buildings commanding a view of the Fiftieth Street exit from the Waldorf Towers were under police surveillance. Windows were to be kept closed.

Consequently there was a moment of acute anxiety, just before the Pope and President emerged, when a police officer shouted through a bullhorn: "Close that window." There was a sudden scurrying about of security personnel. Then somewhere a window slammed shut. It was but one of several such incidents.

Security measures intensified the numbing effects of the Pope's visit on city traffic. All movement of airplanes at Kennedy International Airport was banned for about twenty-five minutes after the Pope's arrival at 9:27 A.M. East River traffic was frozen for half an hour before the Pope's scheduled crossing of the Queensborough Bridge. Motor traffic in Queens and upper Manhattan was paralyzed as police closed off intersections long in advance of the arrival of the motorcade.

But it was a day when everything seemed to go well. The crowds were huge but by and large they were orderly.

Hundreds of thousands of parochial-school children were moved safely to and from the route of the papal motorcade, thanks to thorough advance preparations. Transit Authority buses and chartered buses carried children to previously allocated areas. Each of the more than four hundred parochial

2

schools in the city knew precisely where its children would be deployed along the route.

This vast movement was completed before the peak of the morning rush hour. But it meant that the children often had to stand for more than two hours in the cold wind waiting for the motorcade.

It was wintry at the airport when the Pope arrived. A sharp northwest wind nagged at the topcoats of a welcoming party that included United Nations Secretary-General U Thant, General Assembly President Amintore Fanfani, Secretary of State Dean Rusk, Governor Rockefeller and Mayor Wagner. Four of the five American cardinals—Francis Spellman of New York, James Francis McIntyre of Los Angeles, Richard Cushing of Boston and Lawrence Shehan of Baltimore—were also on hand. Joseph Cardinal Ritter remained in Rome at Ecumenical Council Vatican II.

The Pontiff, white-robed and wearing a crimson cape and crimson hat with gold embroidery, stepped from the plane at 9:30 A.M. The airport crowd saw a sparely built man of sixty-eight, with a clifflike forehead and penetrating, deeply set eyes, whose rather formidable gaze was softened by a persistent smile. He stepped gingerly down the ramp after a brief greeting from Secretary-General U Thant. Donning spectacles, and with the Secretary-General at his side, he read an arrival statement in English. The wind ruffled the papers in his hand. The Pope, apparently feeling the cold, read rapidly and almost in a monotone.

"Greetings to you, America!" the Pontiff said. "God bless this land of yours!"

After the brief ceremony the Pope mounted a specially constructed open limousine, sitting on an elevated throne with Cardinal Spellman at his left.

But even before the motorcade left the terminal, it was decided that the weather was too chilly for an open car. The procession stopped and the Pope shifted from the open car into a limousine with a plastic bubble-top. The limousine has 320 horsepower and can go over 100 miles an hour. But through most of the twenty-four mile route through Queens and upper Manhattan it purred along below twenty miles an hour.

Even this was too fast for the chilled crowds who had waited so long for the Pope and saw him only as a passing blur, if their eyes caught him at all.

The day was radiantly bright and in the dry, sparkling air

the skyscrapers of New York were glimpsed by the Pope long before his motorcade reached the East River.

The Pope was never out of sight of schoolchildren and seldom out of earshot of scores of uniformed school bands along the route. The police estimated that 630,000 saw the Pope pass through the bedroom suburbs of Queens, that 319,000 more saw him in Manhattan, while 165,000 waited outside St. Patrick's. By the end of the day, they estimated, 3.8 million people saw the Pope in the city.

Across Queensborough Bridge and into Manhattan, the Pope's first glimpse of the East Side took in the antique shops, fashionable boutiques, big new luxury apartments and remodeled brownstones of Third Avenue. The motorcade paused briefly in front of the Foundling Hospital, just long enough for the Pope to wave to a choir of nuns singing on a reviewing stand, then went on past the beerhalls of Yorkville and into Spanish Harlem, an almost solidly Catholic neighborhood where the cheering was especially warm.

Harlem's streets had never looked so clean; the Department of Sanitation had swept up the litter. But nothing could hide from the Pope's eyes the endless dreary blocks of rotting tenements.

On the turn west into 125th Street, the Pope saw the heart of Negro Harlem. The route passed under the dilapidated 125th Street station of the New York Central Railroad and turned south on Seventh Avenue for the final mile of Harlem, a tolerably well-kept stretch of brownstones running down to Central Park.

The motorcade entered the park at 110th Street. Then down through the length of the park with its fading foliage, patchy, drought-seared meadows only partly revived by recent rains, past the lake and southward toward the midtown skyline. All along the West Drive there were crowds of children, some waving flags and applauding, others standing in awed silence.

As his motorcade emerged from the park, the Pope's view of midtown was through the canyon of Seventh Avenue toward distant Times Square. At Fifty-seventh Street the motorcade swung east past Carnegie Hall through an area of smart shops and art galleries. Here the crowds were thicker.

Fifth Avenue, then, where the sidewalks were jammed from curb to building line.

In front of St. Patrick's Cathedral and for several blocks up and down Fifth Avenue, the police allowed the throng to spill out on the roadway, keeping two lanes clear for the

4

motorcade. Many in the crowd had waited since dawn. The crowds filled the side streets and pressed against Saks Fifth Avenue, where windows were shielded with plywood as a precaution against surging crowds.

The arrival at St. Patrick's brought an emotional welcome. Applause and cheers met the Pope when he mounted the steps of the Gothic edifice and was greeted by church officials at the monumental bronze door.

He started slowly up the center aisle and the congregation of four thousand invited guests erupted in a clamor of cheering that nearly drowned out the sonorous organ notes of the Papal March.

There was a subdued moment while the Pope knelt before the high altar and offered a personal prayer of thanksgiving for a safe journey. Then, after a brief greeting by Cardinal Spellman, the cheering began again. A priest stood on a kneeling bench and shouted, "Long Live the Pope!" Even the nuns on the side aisles joined the cheering.

There was a sudden hush as the Pope, in halting English, responded to Cardinal Spellman's greeting and intoned, in resonant Latin, the papal blessing. Among the congregation were Governor and Mrs. Nelson A. Rockefeller, Mayor and Mrs. Robert F. Wagner, Senator and Mrs. Robert F. Kennedy, Senator Edward M. Kennedy and Speaker of the House John W. McCormack.

The Pope emerged from the north transept door and showed himself to the crowd on Fifty-first Street. *"Papa, Papa, Papa,"* shouted the throng. The Pope walked around the exterior, waving from the terrace. He then disappeared from the crowd through the rear door of the Cardinal's residence.

It was 12:45 P.M. when the Pope, once more riding in a bubble-topped limousine, arrived at the Fiftieth Street entrance of the Waldorf Towers.

Accompanied by Lloyd Hand, United States Protocol Chief, and Cardinal Spellman, the Pope walked on a red carpet to an elevator and was whisked to the 35th-floor Presidential Suite.

President Johnson had been in the suite all morning, occasionally watching the papal motorcade on television. Vice-President Humphrey and Secretary Rusk were with him when the Pope came. Greetings were exchanged. Then the President, wearing a black single-breasted suit and a black tie, and wearing a Silver Star ribbon in his lapel, escorted the Pontiff into a small sitting room for their private talk. They were joined only by two interpreters—Monsignor Paul Marcinkus of the

5

Vatican Secretariat of State and José Deseabra of the State Department—and by Bill Moyers, the President's press secretary.

They spoke of world troublespots. The Pope hoped for an end of the war in Vietnam, but according to Mr. Moyers, he made no specific recommendations for action.

The controversial issue of whether the United States should establish diplomatic relations with the Vatican did not come up, Mr. Moyers said.

The talk turned to the United Nations. The President believed that the Pope's mission came at a strategic moment, that it was part of a general resurgence of the organization in recent months. The visit would be "a significant milestone not only in the life of the United Nations, but in the overriding and over-all quest for peace by all nations," Mr. Moyers quoted the President as saying.

Immediately after the meeting the President flew back to Washington.

Pope Paul returned to the Cardinal's residence while a crowd of one thousand outside began chanting "We want the Pope." The police tried to quiet the crowd by shouting through bullhorns that the Pontiff would not emerge until he went to the United Nations.

At 3:07 P.M. the Pope departed on his main errand: to plead for peace and disarmament before the temporal leaders of the earth.

To an audience that included a glittering array of world diplomats he pleaded for increased trust in the authority and ultimate goals of the United Nations.

Every seat in the high-domed United Nations Assembly chamber was filled except six—and the six empty seats belonged to the delegation from Communist Albania.

The Pope received a thirty-second ovation when he entered the chamber and a standing ovation when he finished his speech. Andrei A. Gromyko, the Soviet Foreign Minister, joined in the applause; later, at a United Nations' reception, the Pope detained Mr. Gromyko for a moment in an apparently cordial conversation.

In the front row of the distinguished visitors' section sat Mrs. John F. Kennedy. She blinked rapidly, fighting back tears, when the Pontiff quoted the words of the late President Kennedy: "Mankind must put an end to war, or war will put an end to mankind."

From the United Nations, the Pope journeyed to nearby

Holy Family Church in West Forty-seventh Street for an inter-faith audience for 120 Protestants, Jews and Catholics selected for their devotion to the ideals of United Nations. The Pope assured them that "the work of peace is not restricted to one religious belief, it is the work and duty of every human person, regardless of his religious conviction."

When he arrived at Yankee Stadium to celebrate mass, ninety thousand people gave the Pope an ovation.

"Peace be to this house, to this continent, and to all those who inhabit it!" he told the chilled throng. "We must love peace, we must make our own the cause of peace. . . ."

As the mass ended and the Pope left, the sports arena resounded to the chant: "Long live the Pope, long live the Pope."

The Pope's last stop in his crowded day was a visit to the Vatican Pavilion at the World's Fair.

Fifty thousand were huddled in the night chill of 38 degrees when the papal motorcade entered the grounds. A fireworks display lit the sky and a recording of the bells of St. Peter's tolled through the public-address system.

The Pope entered the Vatican Pavilion and viewed Michael-angelo's *Pietà* illumined by blue lights. He said a brief prayer in the Chapel of the Good Shepherd on the second floor. Then, in a voice choked with emotion he called out to the crowd from the balcony: "Goodbye, goodbye."

The Pope arrived at Kennedy Airport at 11:03 P.M. Mayor Wagner handed him a vellum scroll conferring honorary citizenship of New York.

Before he walked aboard the plane, the Pontiff in a brief statement said he would never forget the "enthusiastic and affectionate welcome" he had received.

"God bless America!" he exclaimed. "God bless you all!"

7

The Longest Day

By John Cogley

The longest day in Pope Paul VI's life began very early. Shortly before 4 A.M., he celebrated mass in his private chapel at the Vatican. October 4 in the Roman Catholic calendar is the feast of St. Francis of Assisi. During the mass the Pontiff recited prayers particularly designed to recall the virtues of the Saint of Peace and Brotherly Love.

At the same time the seven cardinals and five archbishops who were traveling with the Pontiff were celebrating their own masses in the dark of the Roman night.

The Pope's physician, his valet, the Jesuit Director of Vatican Radio, and the lay director of *Observatore Romano,* the Vatican daily newspaper, completed the official party. Special guests were the official Vatican photographer and the director of Alitalia Airlines.

The second-class passengers on Alitalia Flight 2,800—Rome to New York—were a much less sedate group. There were sixty journalists aboard, only two of whom were women. No stewardesses were assigned to the flight. "We don't use stewardesses for papal flights," a spokesman for Alitalia explained in a tone that suggested the airline is rapidly becoming used to such flights.

The newsmen, representing the world's press, radio and television, arrived before anyone else at the Leonardo da Vinci Airport at Fiumicino on the outskirts of Rome. When they straggled in, one by one, red-eyed and bleary, the airport was still as lonely as any small town bus station in the early hours.

It looked at Fiumicino as if October 4 might be just another day. There was a family stretched out uncomfortably on a hard wooden bench, mother, father and cherubic five-year-old sleeping. Near them was a clutch of Italian nuns reading their matins in a soft whisper. They were led by a determined mother superior who took no chances on their not being on hand when the Pope left to bring his message to the world. The nuns spent the night in the waiting room.

8

But these nuns were not typical of the people of Rome, even of the nuns of Rome. Most Romans stayed home and slept. The Pope left in a blaze of klieg lights and was formally saluted by soldiers and officials as he stepped into the plane. But there were no cheering masses to bid him godspeed. They were to come when he returned to the city at a more reasonable hour.

Moments before boarding his plane in Rome, Pope Paul VI gave a forecast of the plea for world peace that he was to make to the United Nations.

"The world awaits and asks for peace; the world needs peace; the world demands peace—true, stable, durable—after the sufferings of the wars which have disrupted our century, after the immense sorrows that have devastated humanity," he said.

The Pontiff called for an end to mutual enmities and for the settlement of issues through "equable and courageous negotiations" to assure the orderly progress of civil life and the "flowering of free activity of thought and the arts."

"Only peace can guarantee this. And it is peace we ask for with a voice that has no force of arms but is invigorated by the very strength of the Prince of Peace, whose minister and representative on earth we are," the Pope added.

As the Pope's plane flew across the Atlantic, the 2,200 members of the Roman Catholic hierarchy remaining behind in the Vatican to continue the work of the Ecumenical Council prayed at a special mass in St. Peter's Basilica that his mission might point the world's way to peace for "the family of nations."

The plane was scheduled to depart at 5:30 A.M., Rome time. It missed by only two minutes. The weather was good for flying, the crew was handpicked for its skill.

Throughout the trip, there was an immense difference between the first-class and cabin passengers. In the front all was ecclesiastical decorum. In the rear, there was a constant hubbub.

The newsmen were hungry for details and hung on every word of the ship's officers' reports on what was going on behind the closed doors, as if the future of the world depended on what Pope Paul VI had for breakfast. The cameramen constantly jockeyed for position in case the Pontiff decided to visit their crowded quarters.

Twice during the crossing he decided to do so. Two hours after the plane was aloft, the Pope visited the newsmen, nodding and smiling but, in his shyness, barely managing a single

9

word. Camera lights flashed and in four languages passengers were asked to duck, to move to the left or the right, to bow their heads—to make it possible for the moving Pope to come into the cameramen's focus. Throughout, the Pontiff remained unperturbed.

The second time he came round, four hours later, he gave each person aboard a commemorative medal struck for the occasion. In Latin it reminded all that "peace is the child of love."

The Pontiff seemed calm despite what must have been an unaccustomed hubbub. After the Holy Land and India, though, he can no longer be surprised by the insistence of those who have deadlines to meet, columns to fill and pictures to provide. He looked refreshed and fit, as everyone noted, and, remarkably enough, physically prepared for the marathon activity that lay ahead.

But his visits to the second-class section were brief and almost wordless. Before returning to his private room on the plane, he permitted the photographers to come one at a time for more formal pictures. What they were looking for, though, were candid shots, and these possibilities were extremely limited.

Pope Paul VI is a man of resounding dignity and gravity. In his presence the hush seems utterly natural. No man seems less adapted to the fuss and flurry of modern publicity. It seemed evident to those who caught brief glimpses of him as he crossed the Atlantic on his mission of peace that his hour of glory was also an hour of special trial and that deep within himself he might have envied those popes who described themselves as "prisoners of the Vatican," even while he knew his mission is to go out to the world.

A Shout in the Cathedral

BY PAUL L. MONTGOMERY

The white-haired priest stood on the wooden seat of his cathedral pew and, probably for the first time in his life, shouted in church. "Long live the Pope!" he cried, pounding his companion on the shoulders in excitement. "Long live the Pope!"

It was 11:44 A.M. and Pope Paul VI, Supreme Pontiff of the Universal Church, Vicar of Jesus Christ, Patriarch of the West, was walking slowly up the main aisle of St. Patrick's Cathedral in the heart of Manhattan.

Around the slight, calm, white-clad figure there swirled a medley of noises—the huge cathedral organ playing the Papal March, the pealing of the cathedral bells, the applause and shouts of the four thousand invited guests in the vast edifice, the fading cheers of the fifty thousand who had greeted him outside on Fifth Avenue, the murmured prayers of the faithful.

Through it all was a mood that was to follow the Pontiff throughout his day in the city—a current of excitement, a tingling of human electricity, an attitude of unspoken admiration and respect that New Yorkers reserve for a chosen few.

St. Patrick's, the Pope's first stop on his historic visit, is probably the city's best-known church. The gray stone Gothic edifice, begun on August 15, 1859, and finished on May 25, 1879, is the focus of the Easter parade and many other events in the city's life. Early in the afternoon on November 22, 1963, for example, the cathedral filled as if by magic when it became known that the President of the United States was shot. The faith of the worshipers made no difference on that day of sorrow, nor did it make any difference on the day when Pope Paul VI made his visit.

The cathedral, named for the patron saint of the Roman Catholic Archdiocese of New York, occupies a whole tree-shaded block between Fifth and Madison Avenues and 50th and 51st Streets. At the two corners on Madison Avenue are the residences of the cathedral staff and of the Cardinal Archbishop of New York; the other three sides are fronted by a broad promenade.

The cathedral and the adjoining Cardinal's residence, where the Pope refreshed himself and took a brief meal, had probably the most stringent security precautions of all, and with good reason. Last year a fire bomb had been thrown through a basement window in the residence, starting a small blaze in a maid's room. This spring there were three incidents: a Molotov cocktail was hurled at the main altar, burning a woman who was kneeling there in prayer; another fire bomb was found unexploded in a pew; and the glass case around a wax effigy of Pope Pius XII in the cathedral foyer was shattered by a stone.

For a week before the Pope's arrival city policemen were on duty at the cathedral and residence. Every corner of the buildings was searched and searched again.

The Pope had been to St. Patrick's twice before—in September, 1951, when he was Monsignor Giovanni Battista Montini and visited the United States as a tourist, and in June, 1960, when as Cardinal Archbishop of Milan he came to accept an honorary degree from the University of Notre Dame. But his third visit is the one New York will remember.

A hardy few took their places behind the police barricades outside the cathedral on Sunday night, more than twelve hours before the Pope was expected. By 6 A.M. Monday morning there were several hundred gathered on Fifth Avenue in the chill dawn. The thermometer was in the mid-forties. Many of those who came early to get good vantage points were nuns.

By 11 A.M. about fifty thousand people were lining the streets around the cathedral. A police sound truck in their midst bawled out instructions: "Everybody behind the barricades. Please do not push. Please do not shove. Everybody behind the barricades."

At 11:40, on a rising tide of shouts and excitement, the Pontiff pulled up before St. Patrick's. The crowds strained forward. The police were hard-pressed to hold them back.

He climbed the wide steps to the cathedral entrance and turned to wave to the multitudes. Auxiliary Bishop Joseph F. Flannelly, the administrator of the cathedral, greeted him and ushered him through the bronze doors into the sanctuary. He walked slowly down the 300-foot central aisle, gesturing mildly as the congregation applauded and cheered.

The alabaster main altar and the choir in front of it were banked with white and yellow chrysanthemums. Papal chamberlains in scarlet cutaways and gold-trimmed black trousers stood by, as did the ten cardinals in the Pope's party. The prelates—Cicognani and Agaganian of the Roman Curia, Tisserant of France, Gilroy of Australia, Doi of Tokyo, Rugambwa of Africa, Caggiano of Buenos Aires, McIntyre of Los Angeles, Cushing of Boston and Shehan of Baltimore—had celebrated mass at portable altars in the cathedral basement before the Pope's arrival.

In the front row of the congregation were Mayor and Mrs. Robert F. Wagner and Speaker of the House of Representatives John McCormack and his wife. In the row behind were Senator and Mrs. Robert F. Kennedy, Governor and Mrs. Nelson A. Rockefeller, Senator Edward M. Kennedy and many other dignitaries.

Monsignor Francis X. Duffy, director of information for the cathedral, had told the congregation before the Pope's arrival that they were free to respond as they chose. "We are not making any announcement concerning your reaction to the Pope's

12

arrival," he said. "We leave that to your own emotions or devotions."

As photographers' camera lights flashed, Pope Paul VI knelt briefly on a white satin cushion inside the altar rail to pray, then took his place on the pontifical throne emblazoned with his coat-of-arms. The applause continued as Francis Cardinal Spellman walked to a microphone before the congregation. The Pope sat serenely, his hands clasped in his lap.

The Cardinal, a small figure in red and black who walked haltingly to the microphone, welcomed the Pontiff.

"Most Holy Father," he said. "No words are adequate and surely none are necessary to express our heartfelt gratitude for this historic visit of Your Holiness to the United Nations, to our country and to this Cathedral of St. Patrick. We who are privileged to be here today are but a symbolic representation of all those on this continent and throughout the world who join themselves prayerfully in mind and heart to the plea of Your Holiness for peace.

"We pray that the power of the spirit of God may be with you, dear Holy Father, as you voice our pleas to spare all people from the scourge of wars and grant to all mankind the heavenly blessing of peace."

An assistant, Monsignor Mario Naselli Rocca de Corneliano, the Pope's maestro de camera, handed the Pontiff a pair of rimless spectacles. The Pope put them on and walked to the microphone. Reading slowly from a sheet of paper, he replied to the Cardinal's welcome.

Then, again to applause, he gave the papal blessing. Donning a scarlet cape, he walked with Cardinal Spellman outside and around the cathedral as the crowd waved and cheered and shouted, "Papa, Papa, Papa." Then he retired to the residence for a brief rest before his visit with President Johnson.

For the rest of the day crowds filed into the cathedral to touch the floor where the Pope had walked or look at the pillow where he had knelt in prayer. Some furtively plucked flowers from the blossoms massed around the altar to press in their missals and remind them and their children of the historic day.

A Talk With the President

By Tom Wicker

President Johnson conferred with Pope Paul VI at a private forty-six-minute meeting and emerged with the declaration that the Pope's visit to the New World and his address to the United Nations "may be just what the world needs to get us thinking on how to achieve peace."

The President said that he and the Roman Pontiff had exchanged views in a "stimulating and inspiring conversation" about world peace and the betterment of man.

The talk between Mr. Johnson and Pope Paul VI—the fourth in history between an American president and a pope—was conducted in a small room in the Presidential Suite at the Waldorf-Astoria Hotel. The two men sat in large lemon-silk antique chairs, accompanied only by two interpreters and Bill D. Moyers, the press secretary at the White House.

No specific proposals were exchanged, but the conversation touched on a number of issues. In the briefing held later by Mr. Moyers and in the statements issued on behalf of the President and the Pope it was disclosed that the talk covered these topics:

¶ *The India-Pakistan Dispute.* Both men praised the United Nations for its role in arranging an official ceasefire in the conflict over Kashmir.

¶ *The Dominican Republic.* The President expressed appreciation for the efforts of the Papal Nuncio in Santo Domingo in helping establish a ceasefire.

¶ *South Vietnam.* The Pope included South Vietnam as one of the places where dangerous tensions had arisen and where he hoped progress might be made toward peace.

¶ *Alliance for Progress.* Mr. Johnson discussed some of the details of the program and the Pope offered his personal approval and his church's gratitude to the United States for "not merely talking but moving ahead" to the objectives of social improvement in Latin America.

¶ *Literacy.* Views were exchanged on what might be done to help educate the millions of people in the world who cannot read or write. This discussion included comments on ways to increase the life expectancy of millions of the underprivileged throughout the world.

¶ *Civil Rights.* The Pope expressed his appreciation for progress in the United States in civil rights, and Mr. Johnson observed that "leaders in justice" in this country had been heartened by the recent appointment of a Negro as Auxiliary Bishop of New Orleans.

After the talk, the President and the Pope posed for photographs in a sitting room of the Presidential Suite, 35-H, and each delivered a brief statement to the press. Then Mr. Johnson presented his wife and his Roman Catholic daughter, Luci Baines, to the Pope.

Each man also presented members of his official party to the other. Then Mr. Johnson accompanied Pope Paul VI to the East Fiftieth Street entrance of the Waldorf, where thousands of spectators were able to catch a brief glimpse of two of the world's most influential leaders.

Millions more saw their parting on television. Mr. Johnson, smiling broadly, shook hands three times with the Pope, the last time taking the Pontiff's hand in both of his.

As the Pope's limousine pulled away, Mr. Johnson—who towered above the glass roof of the auto—held out his hand directly above the Pope's head, almost as though extending his own form of blessing to the spiritual leader of millions of Roman Catholics.

During the talk the Pope expressed the gratitude of the church for Mr. Johnson's domestic political programs concerning health and education.

As Mr. Johnson put it, "His Holiness expressed his pleasure at our not only talking about education and health but our acting on it in this country."

The Pope's statement following his conversation with Mr. Johnson was delivered in Italian. His interpreter, Monsignor Paul Marcinkus, translated it as follows:

> *His Holiness says he has come here to pay his respects to the President of the United States and also to repay the visit of his predecessor [President John F. Kennedy] to Pope John XXIII in 1963. And also to thank the President for having made this trip from Washington to New York to meet His Holiness. He is very happy that this discussion has revolved about a mutual desire to work for peace.*

Neither man had been scheduled to speak publicly but when Pope Paul concluded the picture-taking session with these remarks, Mr. Johnson also spoke extemporaneously to reporters, saying:

> *The entire world is indebted to His Holiness, as I said to him in our private conversation, for the sacrifices he has made in coming on this long trip across the water to provide leadership in the world's quest for peace. His Holiness and I discussed ways and means of advancing that cause.*
>
> *We also exchanged views in detail in connection with what could be done to help provide education to the 800 million people of the world who cannot read or write, to help increase the life expectancy of the millions of humans who now die at an early age, with a life expectancy less than half of what it is in this country.*
>
> *We discussed in some detail trouble spots in the world today and the great progress made by the United Nations in trying to provide help in those trouble spots.*
>
> *We discussed India-Pakistan, the Dominican Republic, Vietnam and all the continents generally. It has been to me a very stimulating and inspiring conversation, and I believe that history may well record this venture of His Holiness, this breaking of precedent in coming on this long trip across the water may be just what the world needs to get us thinking on how to achieve peace and getting us to make progress in that area.*

At a later news conference, Mr. Moyers added considerable detail to the President's outline of the talks.

Mr. Moyers said Pope Paul VI had made no specific proposals for bringing peace to South Vietnam.

The press secretary said there had been no discussion at all of birth control, in which the United States government lately has become active. Nor was the idea of United States diplomatic representation at the Vatican raised between the two leaders, he said.

According to Mr. Moyers's account, the President opened the discussion by thanking the Pope for undertaking his tiring mission. Then Mr. Johnson discussed ideas for achieving peace, and for improving health and education on a worldwide basis.

They discussed world racial unrest and American progress in civil rights.

The President told the Pope of having seen Pope John XXIII in 1962—when Mr. Johnson was Vice-President—and of having learned from him that peace was still possible despite the troubles of the world.

A lengthy discussion of the United Nations followed, with the President expressing appreciation for the Pope's visit as an evidence of his great support for the U.N. Mr. Johnson noted a recent U.N. resurgence of strength and said the papal visit (as Mr. Moyers paraphrased it) "would be a significant milestone not only in the life of the U.N. but in the over-riding and over-all quest for peace."

Mr. Johnson discussed the Alliance for Progress and the Pope replied that the Roman Catholic Church, too, was committed to justice, progress and social improvement in Latin America.

Mr. Johnson then said he was aware of the church's interest in education, not only in a general way but through his daughter, Luci, who is a student at the Georgetown University School of Nursing, a Catholic institution in Washington, D. C.

"She keeps me informed," Mr. Johnson said (again, as Mr. Moyers paraphrased his remarks).

The President returned to world peace by saying it could never be achieved until the people of all countries could read, write, have social justice, have their bodies healed of disease, and share in a better life for all.

The Pope replied that his church and the American people had a "common objective" in reaching these goals for all people.

Each man thanked the other for coming to New York and the Pope said he hoped Mr. Johnson would continue with all his optimism and energy to work for peace. When men of the spirit turned to men of affairs for guidance, he said, it was to men like the President that they looked.

Mr. Johnson returned the compliment. When men of affairs sought spiritual guidance, he said, it was to leaders like the Pope that they turned.

The Pope arrived at the Waldorf at 12:35 P.M. He was wearing white, with a red cape, red leather shoes, and a white cap. He arrived in a glass-roofed limousine, riding in the rear seat with Giovanni Cardinal Cicognani, the Papal Secretary of State and formerly the Apostolic Delegate to the United States.

Just before the Pope's arrival, a green carpet was taken away to disclose a red carpet underneath, covering the Fiftieth Street sidewalk and entrance. Two urns of yellow and white chrysanthemums stood at curbside.

The street had been kept generally clear of onlookers, except for reporters and photographers. Crowds were thick nearby on Park and Lexington Avenues.

The sleek glass walls of the I.T.T. building at Fiftieth Street and Park Avenue were crowded with spectators. Two floors

17

above the street, a huddle of Waldorf cooks, wearing chef's hats, peered out a window. A group of nuns looked from a fifth-floor window.

Police had difficulty making some of these spectators keep their windows closed. Three young girls with long blonde hair persisted in leaning out a fifth-floor window despite repeated entreaties and threats from the police.

Just before the Pope's arrival, a window just above sidewalk level opened furtively in the massive stone wall of St. Bartholomew's Episcopal Church. A white-haired gentleman peered out.

The police were quick to spot this violation of security. An officer arrived and politely told the man to close the window.

"But I want to see," the man replied.

"You'll have to close the window," the officer said.

"You'll have to come in and close it," the man in the window replied, somewhat testily. This show of resistance caused the officer to go away peacefully.

As the Pope emerged from his limousine, smiling and giving a two-handed gesture of greeting, windows opened rapidly in the Waldorf façade. Up and down the street, policemen began bellowing, "Close those windows!"—a somewhat bellicose background chorus for the arrival of a seeker of peace.

After the Pope entered the hotel the green carpet quickly went back down on the red. The police relaxed. The windows went up again. Photographers put down their cameras.

At the door to Suite 35–H, the Pope was met by Mr. Johnson, Vice-President Humphrey and Secretary of State Dean Rusk, at 12:40 P.M.

At 12:42, the President and the Pope went into a small room and began their discussions.

José de Seabra of the State Department acted as Mr. Johnson's interpreter. The Pope speaks excellent but accented English and preferred to converse in Italian.

The room in which the conversations took place was small, of English and French decor, with a deep blue rug bordered with a red design. The draperies were of gold and white satin damask and the room was decorated with yellow and white roses and yellow and orange chrysanthemums. Four paintings —two Neapolitan and two pastoral—hung on the walls. The pastorals were by Francis Wheatley and William James Muller.

After their talk, the Pope and the President went to the sitting room of Suite 35–H for a picture-taking session that lasted about four minutes. This room was white-walled, with carpeting, draperies, chairs and couches in a dominant rust color.

The two men sat for their portrait, the Pope on the right, permitting Mr. Johnson to expose his favored left profile to the photographers.

The chairs were arranged before a white marble fireplace, on whose mantel there were two crystal candelabra. Above the fireplace hung a Frederic Remington original, loaned for the occasion by Findlay Galleries of New York.

It depicts a blanketed Indian under a tree, holding a pipe to his lips. It is called *Peace Pipe* by some but is also known as *Love Call*.

Ferns and rhododendrons were arranged in the fireplace.

After reporters and photographers were shown out, Mr. Johnson presented his wife and Luci to the Pope. Mrs. Johnson wore a black silk-and-wool dress and a small black hat. Luci wore a double-breasted, two-piece black wool suit with a straight skirt, long sleeves and a high neck. She also wore a black lace mantilla.

Mr. Johnson then presented to the Pope a number of members of his official party, including the following: Mr. and Mrs. Humphrey, Secretary Rusk, Speaker of the House and Mrs. John W. McCormack, Ambassador and Mrs. Arthur Goldberg, Senator and Mrs. Mike Mansfield, Postmaster-General and Mrs. Lawrence F. O'Brien, Joseph Califano and John J. Valenti of the White House staff, Mrs. Yolande Boozer and Mrs. Dorothy Terito, White House secretaries.

Pope Paul VI introduced Cardinal Cicognani to the President. Others in his party included Archbishop Antonio Samore of the Vatican Secretariat Congregation for Extraordinary Affairs; Archbishop Angelo Dell-Acqua, the Substitute of Secretariat of State; Archbishop Egidio Vagnozzi, the Apostolic Delegate to the United States; Monsignor Marcinkus, and Pasquale Macchi, the personal secretary to the Pope.

The Pope's meeting with Mrs. Johnson and Luci lasted no longer than two minutes.

Downstairs, the green carpet was taken off the red, a porter appeared to sweep the way clean, and the police began shouting again at viewers in open windows.

When the Pope and the President emerged, Mr. Johnson was walking on his left with one arm behind the Pope's back. They shook hands first on the steps, then on the sidewalk, then as the Pope entered his limousine.

Before he did so, Mr. Johnson turned him gently toward Lexington Avenue to face a cluster of photographers and a television camera on the sidewalk.

The Pope constantly recognized the crowds with a two-handed gesture.

After the Pope entered the limousine, Ambassador Hand walked with the elderly Cardinal Cicognani around to the street side of the car. They entered and it drove away, with Mr. Johnson waving after them.

The President did not linger long. He immediately flew back to Washington, where he watched the Pope's speech to the General Assembly on a television set in his White House office.

Other than Mr. Johnson today and President Kennedy in 1963—the day after Pope Paul VI took office—two presidents have had audiences with a Pope. They were Dwight D. Eisenhower, who met with Pope John XXIII on December 6, 1959, and Woodrow Wilson, who saw Pope Benedict XV on January 4, 1919, both in Rome.

Six other presidents had papal audiences either before or after they left office, all in Rome.

Before he became President, Mr. Johnson—then a member of Congress—met Pope Pius XII in Rome on May 26, 1945. On December 7, 1962, as Vice-President, Mr. Johnson met Pope John XXIII in Rome. At the funeral of Pope John XXIII, he was the official American representative, and at that time—June 17, 1963—he was introduced to Giovanni Cardinal Montini, who was elected Pope a few weeks later.

The two men did not meet again until the Pope's visit to New York.

The Pope's Plea: "War Never Again!"

By Drew Middleton

With the dignity of the head of a great and ancient church and the fervor of a simple man seeking peace, Pope Paul VI asked the United Nations to do away with offensive weapons and to build a universal authority.

The Pontiff, a slim figure in white, stood at the green marble rostrum of the General Assembly, and cried in French, "No more war, war never again!"

Before him in the green, gold and blue Assembly Hall were the representatives of 116 of the United Nations' 117 members. Only tiny Albania, Communist China's spokesman in Eastern Europe, boycotted the papal address.

Peace was the dominant theme of Pope Paul VI's message. But he also spoke of the United Nations' working at its best on a basis of universality and he asked the Assembly to "bring back among you" those that have left and to study methods of "uniting to your pact of brotherhood, in honor and loyalty, those who do not yet share in it."

The Pope asked the nations to ensure that there is enough bread "for the tables of mankind" rather than "favor an artificial control of birth, which would be irrational, in order to diminish the number of guests at the banquet of life."

The Pope's choice of bread before birth control was a significant and perhaps decisive contribution to the Catholic Church's debate on birth control. It was delivered to an audience with many members representing the teeming, hungry populations of Africa, Asia and Latin America.

For years a great debate on birth control has raged within the Roman Catholic Church. Although no one could be certain what the Pope's remarks meant for the future of this debate, some diplomats believed it threw his weight, as head of the church, against relaxation of the doctrinal stand against artificial contraception.

To an audience of about 2,200 the Pontiff pledged the authority of the Catholic Church to the United Nations, which he called "the last hope of concord and peace."

He went on from there to stress "the necessity" of progressing to a world authority, "able to act efficaciously on the juridical and political levels."

The Pontiff's address, with its emphasis on universality, disarmament and the development of a world authority, went far beyond the simple plea for peace expected by most delegates.

He was heard in silence. When he finished with an appeal for a restoration of spiritual values in furthering civilization, there was a second of silence and then a long burst of applause. Foreign minister Andrei A. Gromyko of the Soviet Union was as responsive in his reaction at this point as Foreign Minister Maurice Couve de Murville of France.

The Pope's reference to widening the membership of the United Nations went straight to one of the most bitterly debated issues of this General Assembly.

"Those who do not yet share" in the "brotherhood" include

Communist China, whose admission is opposed by the United States and supported by the Soviet Union, France and a number of African and Asian states.

Secretary of State Dean Rusk was listening with Mr. Gromyko and Mr. Couve de Murville when the Pope made his pronouncement.

Others outside the United Nations include West Germany and East Germany. Those "who have separated themselves"—in the Pope's words—include Indonesia, with 100 million people.

The Pontiff's reference to the acute issue of Communist China's admission, oblique though it was, provoked wide discussion among delegates. Two leading Catholic members of the world organization, France and Italy, have advocated Peiping's admission, and the Pope's apparent endorsement seemed to strengthen their position on this issue within the General Assembly.

The United States from the outset has opposed Communist China's admission. American officials, while clinging to their belief that Peiping would be kept out, conceded after the speech that the Pope's support for univeraslity in the world organization would have a significant effect upon many delegations.

Pope Paul VI's diplomatic initiatives were not confined to his plea to the Assembly.

At the end of his stay at the United Nations he talked briefly and separately with four foreign ministers, Michael Stewart of Britain, Mr. Rusk, Mr. Gromyko and Mr. Couve de Murville.

The brief talks, one official said, gave the Pontiff an opportunity to emphasize the importance he placed upon the points, particularly nuclear disarmament, he had raised in his speech to the Assembly.

Long before the Pope's entrance the delegations were in their places in the hall. The majority of Africans and Asians were in dark business suits except for a few in brightly colored robes.

Heads turned when Mrs. John F. Kennedy arrived escorted by Richard Cardinal Cushing and her brothers-in-law, Senators Robert F. Kennedy of New York and Edward M. Kennedy of Massachusetts.

Later, during a reception in the delegates' lounge, Mrs. Kennedy knelt and kissed the Pope's ring. The Pope spoke softly

22

to her for a minute, holding her hands, and Mrs. Kennedy, after a moment, raised her head and smiled.

Amintore Fanfani, Italy's Foreign Minister and the President of the twentieth session of the General Assembly, called the meeting to order and then departed with the Secretary General, U Thant, to escort the Pope down the central aisle to the platform.

As the white-clad figure appeared, the applause began, lasting for nearly a minute until the Pope had reached the platform. He acknowledged the welcome with the already familiar gesture, arms half outstretched as if to grasp every hand in the auditorium.

He sat in a large beige leather chair, last used by President Kennedy, while first Mr. Fanfani and then Mr. Thant welcomed him to the session. The Pope sat motionless.

Seated to the left and right of the platform were the cardinals of the Pope's entourage and of the United States. Their scarlet birettas and sashes added a vivid splash of color.

These princes of the church, representing every continent, were a reminder of the global influence of Pope Paul VI's church. Yet early in his speech, he told the audience that "you have before you a humble man, your brother."

He said it was a great occasion, "great for us, great for you," because he was following the ancient command to his church to "go and bring the good news to all peoples."

For a world organization considered by many to be suffering from a loss of prestige, the Pontiff brought powerful reinforcement. To him the United Nations represented the unmistakable road toward peace.

"Retreat," he said, "must never be admitted."

He saw progress in the admission of "the younger peoples" and in the adoption of the principle of universality, that is, the creation of a United Nations that embraces all countries.

"Go forward always," the Pope advised in beginning what was considered to be the most controversial part of his speech, that which advised the world organization to expand and admit those who had departed and those not yet in. He declared: "Strive to bring back among you any who have separated themselves, and study the right method of uniting to your pact of brotherhood, in honor and loyalty, those who do not yet share in it. Act so that those still outside will desire and merit the confidence of all, and then be generous in granting such confidence."

23

From this the Pontiff passed to an insistence upon the principle of equality among members. All members might not be equal, he said, but in a passage presumably directed to the large powers—the United States and the Soviet Union—he declared that it was an "act of high virtue" to assume equality because man's brotherhood was impossible without humility.

This humility, the Pope indicated, is essential for peace. But peace, he insisted, must be built as much by ideas as with politics and the balance of forces and interests.

The first step, the Pope declared, is disarmament. "Let the arms fall from your hands," he advised the nations, for "one cannot love while holding offensive arms."

Man, "unfortunately," must retain defensive arms, the Pope said, but the starting point is the abandonment of offensive nuclear weapons that poison men's minds, demand enormous expenditures and divert men's efforts from the works of peace.

Pope Paul VI's appeal for outlawing nuclear offensive weapons came at a time when the United States and the Soviet Union, the two great nuclear powers, are deadlocked on the issue.

The Soviet Union demands a ban on the dissemination of nuclear weapons, which, to Moscow, means forbidding nuclear arms to the West Germans. The United States advocates a halt in the production of nuclear weapons and the diversion of fissionable material to peaceable use. Neither government has shown any flexibility.

The Pontiff's broad appeal for the junking of all nuclear weapons appeared to be an attempt to bridge the gap between the two positions and to end the long Soviet-American wrangle over the takeoff point for nuclear disarmament.

The principle of working "one for another" was seen by the Pope as a beacon of hope for the world. He described brotherly cooperation among the peoples as the United Nations at its best.

Respect for human life "even with regard to the great problem of the birth rate" must find in the United Nations its affirmation and its defense, the Pope declared in introducing his comment on birth control.

"You must strive," he said, "to multiply bread so that it suffices for the tables of mankind, and not rather favor an artificial control of births, which would be irrational, in order to diminish the number of guests at the banquet of life."

Man's dignity is as much a necessity as bread, he said, and in this field he praised the United Nation's efforts to hasten social and economic progress by harnessing the resources of science, technology and modern organization.

The Pontiff's final point, however, was that what the world organization did in the future must rest on more than material accomplishments. The hour has come, he emphasized, for inner transformation and renewal, for recollection, reflection and prayer. The dangers, he warned, come not from science but from man, who now has the means of his own destruction.

The audience embraced every faith and every race. Directing it to a revival of spiritual principles, the Pontiff noted that faith in God could be founded upon "the unknown God" of whom St. Paul preached to the Athenians.

"Unknown to them, although without realizing it, they sought him and he was close to them, as happens also to many men of our times," the Pope said.

The speech at the General Assembly was the climax of a visit whose history goes back to 1963 and the reign of Pope John XXIII. A few months before he died in that year Pope John XXIII issued what became the most significant document of his reign, the encyclical entitled "Pacem in Terris" (Peace on Earth).

In 1964 scholars at the Center for the Study of Democratic Institutions at Santa Barbara, California, decided to convene an international conference to study the implications of Pope John XXIII's plea for world order and understanding.

A preliminary planning session for the conference was held in Racine, Wisconsin, in May, 1964. Among those present was C. B. Narasimhan, U Thant's adviser. He suggested that the Secretary-General invite Pope Paul VI to New York for the opening of the conference at the United Nations in February, 1965.

When the Pope attended the International Eucharistic Congress in Bombay, India, he reiterated Pope John XXIII's plea for peace and disarmament. He sent a copy of his remarks to Mr. Thant.

The Secretary-General sent an invitation to the Pope on January 20, 1965.

"Since preserving peace among nations is one of the essential aims of the United Nations," Mr. Thant wrote, "we share the firm and profound desire and resolution of Your Holiness to achieve the end of the arms race among sovereign powers."

"I am ready," Mr. Thant continued, "in the name of the United Nations to study immediately whether it would be possible for Your Holiness to appear before the General Assembly sitting in special meeting during the nineteenth session which is now going on."

For a time there was no answer from the Vatican. It was thought possible that he would come to New York for the conference on "Pacem in Terris" which opened at the United Nations in February, 1965. Apparently, however, the Pope decided to postpone his visit until the fall and the twentieth session, although he sent a personal message of greeting to the conference.

A Word for Everyone

By Raymond Daniell

Pope Paul VI listened and chatted as some five hundred foreign diplomats and distinguished guests were presented to him in the delegates' lounge. For almost everyone, the Pope had a word in French, English or Italian.

Among the many who touched his hand were dark-skinned men from Africa and Asia, representing countries practicing the Muslim or Buddhist religions, and some from countries where witchcraft and animism are still tolerated. Many come from new countries, some with more than one million inhabitants but with fewer than one hundred college graduates—countries just beginning to struggle upward from the direst poverty.

One of the longest colloquies took place between Pope Paul VI and Andrei Gromyko, Foreign Minister of the Soviet Union. Later there was a smaller reception in the suite of U. N. Secretary-General U Thant, on the thirty-eighth floor. There the Pontiff had an opportunity to confer and discuss matters at greater length with Mr. Gromyko, United States Secretary of State Dean Rusk, Roger Seydoux, representative of France, and Lord Caradon, the British representative.

Before departing, the Pope presented Secretary-General Thant a diamond-studded cross and a diamond ring, a gift to the United Nations through its Secretary-General.

They are to be sold and the proceeds used in the world campaign against hunger. The gifts were estimated to be worth $115,000.

The Secretary-General said in accepting them that if the Big Four—the Soviet Union, the United States, France and

Britain—wanted to bid for them he would accept the highest offer.

The Secretary-General presented to the Pope the International Cooperation Year Medal and, as a private gift, a Burmese silver bowl in a wooden case. It was engraved: "He who conquers himself is the greatest of all conquerors," a phrase from Buddhist scripture. It was signed by U Thant and bore the date October 4, 1965.

The Pope also gave the Secretary-General a personal gift. It was a symbol of love and peace, described as a bronze piece shaped like a flame.

Earlier at the reception for the diplomats, Pope Paul VI gave the Secretary-General a painting of the crucifixion by Georges Rouault as a presentation to the United Nations. Thant thanked him on behalf of the world organization.

Immediately after delivering his speech to the General Assembly Pope Paul was escorted through the meeting places of the Security Council, the Trusteeship Council and the Economic and Social Council. In each he delivered little impromptu homilies in French.

Delegates for whom there was not room in the Assembly heard and saw the Pope delivering his speech over closed-circuit television in the Security Council. Members of nongovernmental organizations, composed of citizens who support the United Nations, watched television in the Trusteeship Council. Representatives of the press heard and saw the Pope in the larger Economic and Social Council. They rose and applauded when he entered.

To them, he said: "We wish to thank you for this welcome because it comes from the press. From the press! You know we are a friend of the press."

He added that it was not only because the press had special knowledge of world events but because "You are the word."

He expressed the hope that the press would be able to sustain its burden of responsibility. Upon leaving he said: "We wish to hail you and to congratulate you. We are much impressed by your scholarship and your art."

It was a day like none other at the United Nations, which has witnessed a shoe-thumping Nikita Khrushchev, heard a bearded Fidel Castro fulminate against the United States and has been the scene of many angry and bitter debates in the cold war between East and West. With him the Pope brought an aura of brotherly love and self-abnegation which for a brief time at least touched and moved his auditors.

The room where the big reception was held is a spacious one, with a bar and coffee lounge at one end, a reading nook surrounded by potted palms at the other, and chairs and tables where delegates gather to discuss their problems and conduct "corridor diplomacy."

It is their private club, but in normal times it is somewhat reminiscent of an airplane terminal with delegates being paged in five different languages over a public-address system. Its broad windows look northward over the landscaped gardens of the United Nations and the East River.

Pope Paul VI stood at the west end of the lounge, facing a huge chocolate-colored map of the world that hung at the east end.

As the line formed to be presented to the Pope, two blue-uniformed waitresses and a chef, his tall white hat standing out like a beacon, stood at the entrance to the lounge. Other employees stood on the landings of the escalators on the second floor from which they caught a glimpse of the Pontiff as he made his progress from the small south lounge to the bigger one at the north end of the building.

Foreign Minister Gromyko and Nikolai T. Fedorenko, the Soviet Union's representative, were not the only representatives of Communist countries to bow before the Pope. Others included Raul Roa García, Foreign Minister of Cuba; Vaclav David, Foreign Minister of Czechoslovakia; Ivan Bashev of Bulgaria; Marco Nikezic of Yugoslavia; Ahmed T. Dugerburen of Mongolia; K. V. Kiselev of Byelorussia; and Carneliu Manescu, Foreign Minister of Romania.

Countries whose foreign ministers were not present were represented by their permanent representatives: Bohdan Lewandowski of Poland; Karoly Castorday of Hungary and Sergei T. Shevchenko of the Ukraine. Behar Schtylla, Foreign Minister of Albania, whose speech in the Assembly last week aroused Arthur J. Goldberg, United States Representative, to an angered reply, was not seen at the reception.

Governor Rockefeller of New York and Mrs. Rockefeller; Secretary of State Rusk and Mrs. Rusk; Paul Martin, Minister for External Affairs of Canada and many other representatives of friendly nations were presented. But it was Mrs. Kennedy and Mr. Gromyko who received the most attention from the Pope at the large reception. Later as Mrs. Kennedy and her brothers- and sisters-in-law were leaving, they passed through the Economic and Social Council, and seeing that the proceedings were being shown on a television show, tarried to watch awhile. They left by the escalator that led to the delegates' entrance, to the delight of a crowd that had gathered there.

Upon his arrival at the United Nations, Pope Paul VI, who rode with Cardinal Spellman, was greeted by the Secretary-General inside the seven doors to the Assembly Hall donated by Canada. Before the Pope spoke to the General Assembly the Secretary-General escorted him on a brief visit to the meditation room. Its V-shaped chamber is thirty by eighteen feet with only a stone slab waist high in the middle and an unobtrusive mural of geometric figures to distract attention.

It was designed, as the late Dag Hammarskjold said, as "a room of quiet where only thoughts should speak. It is a room of stillness where nothing intrudes on those who wish to find stillness; a place where doors may be opened to infinite lands of thoughts and prayers."

From there the Pope proceeded to the Assembly, entering the floor from the rear and walking down the center aisle to the podium, holding his hands before him with upraised palms.

The Other Faiths

BY GEORGE DUGAN

Pope Paul VI's plea for peace had a dramatic ecumenical echo at Holy Family Roman Catholic Church, the newest edifice in the far-flung New York Archdiocese.

There, on East 47th Street, half a block from United Nations Plaza, the Pontiff told nearly a hundred Protestant, Eastern Orthodox and Jewish guests that the search for peace was the "work and duty of every human person, regardless of his religious conviction."

The Pope arrived at the ultracontemporary church at 6:20 P.M., nearly an hour after the arrival of Cardinal Spellman.

He was welcomed by Monsignor Timothy J. Flynn, pastor of Holy Family, turned to bless the crowds on 47th Street, and then walked slowly up the aisle.

Despite tight security, a seven-year-old lad slipped under the arms of a guard, knelt and kissed the papal ring.

The Pope patted the youngster's head, smiled and moved on to a chair in front of the church's plain black marble altar.

The little worshiper was Frederick Henderson, son of a member of the United Nations security staff.

More than three hundred persons filled the sanctuary of the church as well as an adjoining room opened for the occasion.

Forty Protestant and Eastern Orthodox representatives sat on the Pope's right, across the middle aisle from an equal number of Roman Catholics.

The forty-eight Jewish guests filled the adjoining room, most of them there in deference to their traditional ban on participating in a religious ceremony of another faith.

The rest of the congregation was made up of Holy Family parishioners and persons affiliated with the United Nations.

Before the Pope began his brief address, Monsignor Flynn told the Pontiff that all the visitors were "united with Your Holiness in your historic mission for peace and express to your Holiness their profound pleasure and their heartfelt welcome."

Andrew Cordier, dean of the Graduate School of International Affairs of Columbia University and chairman of the Protestant and Eastern Orthodox Church Center for the United Nations, then spoke for his coreligionists.

A member of the Church of the Brethren, Mr. Cordier called the Holy Family gathering a "historic meeting" of religious leaders dedicated to the cause of world peace.

"With the hope of a new brotherly spirit in the world," he said, "we believe new opportunities can come for all who serve the God of love to make increasing contributions to His purpose for friendship, freedom, truth, justice and order.

"To these ends, as workers together with one another and with God, we pledge our renewed and deepening dedication to pray, study, think and act cooperatively in pursuing peace for a more harmonious and abundant life for all races and nations of men in God's human family."

The Jewish spokesman, Philip Klutznick, former United States representative to the United Nations Social and Economic Council, spoke in similar vein.

He came to the altar from his seat in the front row of Jewish guests in the adjoining room.

"During this hour of trial for humanity, as mankind faces continuous crises, your meeting with representatives of the faith communities give new promise for the future," Mr. Klutznick declared.

"As a people whose ideal is 'sholom, peace,' we pledge our untiring efforts to help promote peace in every dimension, political, social and economic.

"Your presence here is one more meaningful manifestation of the moral and spiritual basis indispensable to a lasting peace with truth and justice—which material and finite resources alone cannot achieve."

After their comments, the spokesmen stood together and presented the Pope with an illuminated scroll bearing this inscription from Isaiah 2:4: "And they shall beat their swords into plowshares, and their spears into pruning hooks; nation shall not lift up sword against nation, neither shall they learn war any more."

The Pontiff then rose and voiced his "distinct pleasure" at meeting with the varied religious groups.

Reading in English and gesturing repeatedly with his left hand, the Pontiff promised cooperation with them in religion's search for peace.

"In a way," he asserted, "we have left our purely spiritual sphere of activity in order to know your work for peace, to which you are dedicating yourselves so earnestly, and to collaborate with you insofar as it is possible for us, and to associate ourselves in a certain measure with your efforts."

Some seventeen Protestant bodies were represented at the church. Along with the Jews and the Roman Catholics all the guests were involved in one way or another with the United Nations.

Holy Family Church was dedicated March, 1965, by Cardinal Spellman as a "parish center to serve the spiritual needs of the United Nations community" and to minister to residents of the Turtle Bay area.

The gleaming gray granite structure was built on what was once the site of an old brewery stable. In 1925 it was converted into a church.

When plans were formulated to rehabilitate the edifice a few of the old parishioners rebelled at the idea of change and resented its transformation into a United Nations parish.

All of them have apparently accepted Holy Family's "renewal," according to Monsignor Flynn, the forty-eight-year-old pastor who is also director of the archdiocesan bureau of information.

The parish complex includes a rectory, the residence of Monsignor Alberto Giovannetti, permanent observer of the Holy See to the United Nations, and the Pope John XXIII Pacem in Terris multilingual library.

It also houses the offices of Roman Catholic organizations working with the United Nations.

There was unanimous agreement among the Protestant observers that the papal visit to Holy Family constituted a landmark in the growing rapprochement with Roman Catholics.

Methodist Bishop James K. Matthews of Boston saw in the visit a "living symbol" of the growth of the ecumenical movement.

So did Episcopal Bishop William Crittenden of Erie, Pennsylvania, who hailed the papal pilgrimage as a harbinger of closer cooperation between the two great branches of Christendom.

Ninety Thousand Amens

By William E. Farrell

Under the brilliant glare of floodlights at Yankee Stadium, 90,000 people had their eyes riveted at a spot 171 feet from home plate.

There, on a red-carpeted platform in a sanctuary topped by an octagonal canopy of gold canvas, Pope Paul VI stood in the cold night before a plain wooden altar covered with a simple white linen cloth and celebrated the central act of worship for the Roman Catholic Church—the mass.

It was the first time that a pope had celebrated on American soil the centuries-old ritual that is a re-creation in words and symbols of the crucifixion of Jesus.

The crowd, including about three thousand Jews, Protestants and Orthodox, began trickling into the huge sports stadium in the Bronx when the gates were opened at 3 P.M.

At that time the Pontiff was preparing to leave Cardinal Spellman's residence for the United Nations to address the General Assembly. It would be five hours and thirty-seven minutes before he would appear in the stadium in an open convertible driven through the gate of the left-field bullpen, where the visiting baseball teams' relief pitchers warm up.

Hawkers were everywhere, their cries piercing the air, selling documentary phonograph records of the Pope's visit to the Holy Land, pennants, statues of the Infant of Prague, crucifixes, rosaries, buttons with the Pope's likeness above a bit of ribbon, key chains embossed with the papal tiara, and color photographs in all sizes of the Pontiff.

The stadium was arrayed in white and gold silk bunting, the papal colors. The advertisements on the walls behind the bleachers were obliterated by hundreds of yards of billowing blue cloth. Clusters of small flags of the member nations of the United Nations were everywhere and atop the stadium's huge flagpoles the United Nations, United States and papal colors fluttered.

Thousands of gold and white chrysanthemums and greens were placed around the six-and-a-half-foot-high platform that held the pulpit, a three-foot-high altar, and a prie-dieu, or kneeler.

The only stone in the sanctuary was a small altar stone, about nine inches long and nine inches wide, containing the relics—usually bone—of a saint.

In the outfield, in front of the bleachers, a picket fence was used to rope off an area for students, who as early as 5 P.M. stood clad in warm coats, huddled together. Many had forgotten to wear gloves and blew on their hands or clasped hot containers of coffee in both hands.

Earmuffs, gaudy Indian blankets and brightly colored women's coats were everywhere, contrasting sharply with the patches of black throughout the stadium that told where the thousands of priests and nuns were seated.

Several nuns were wearing modern habits, a recent innovation in the church. They were long blue coats that buttoned down the front, with blue cowls attached, and modified headdresses. One young nun, wearing a borrowed khaki trenchcoat over her shoulders, nonchalantly ate a hot-dog.

Officials of the Knights of Columbus paraded about in white-lined black capes. Tricorn hats with white plumage completed their outfits.

Two front rows of seats facing the altar were set aside for the papal party, which included eleven cardinals. Each of the church dignitaries had his own prie-dieu. Behind them sat dozens of monsignors, wearing flowing red capes and black birettas with red pompoms. Many of the some 225 American bishops were in Rome for Ecumenical Council Vatican II and did not attend the service.

By 8 P.M. the stadium was jammed. To pass the time until the Pope's arrival the Princeton University Pro Musica Brass Ensemble, a group specializing in the vast repository of sacred brass music begun in Renaissance Italy four hundred years ago, offered a prelude consisting of *Ricercare sopra li Tuoni* by Palestrina, a sixteenth-century organist and composer; a *Pavane* by Thilman Susato, a sixteenth-century Dane; *Sechs Psalmensätze* by Heinrich Schütz, a seventeenth century German, and a Palestrina motet, *Tu Es Pastor Ovium*, the test of which refers to the Pontiff as the successor to St. Peter and "the shepherd of My flock."

As the moment for the Pope to enter neared, the snack bars shut down, the hawkers' voices stilled, cigarettes were put out and women anxiously patted their heads to be sure their hats covered their crowns.

The stadium slowly assumed the aura of a church.

The cinder track around the baseball field was cleared, conversations grew quieter, hundreds of policemen fixed their eyes on the crowds. Around the track dozens and dozens of policemen faced the throngs, their backs to the altar. They had been forbidden by Police Commissioner Vincent L. Broderick to peer at the historic proceeding.

At 8:34 an announcement over the public-address system said that the papal motorcade was outside the stadium. Three minutes later, to restrained, then tumultuous applause, the slender pontiff, dressed in a long white cassock, red cape and white zucchetto, or skullcap, entered the stadium, standing in his limousine, his right hand extended in greeting.

For the next six minutes, the Pontiff circled the stadium's cinder path, evoking separate waves of applause from each section he passed that sounded as if a huge conch shell were being repeatedly pressed to the ear, then rapidly withdrawn.

Seated next to the Pontiff was Cardinal Spellman, Archbishop of New York and the Pope's host. A large group of uniformed and plainclothes security police trotted alongside the open car.

After circling the stadium one and a half times, the car halted before a red carpet than ran between two rows of spectators' seats and covered home plate.

When the Pope, ducking with some difficulty the top of the car door, alighted, the stadium erupted for the first time in unanimous applause and cheers.

Arms outstretched, his hands turned toward his chest, fingers bending toward palms, the Pope strode briskly along the carpet toward the altar.

There were cries of *"Viva! Viva!"*

At the foot of the altar he paused, then mounted the thirteen steps to the square platform that held the sanctuary. As he knelt at his prie-dieu, 225 seminarians from the nine major seminaries in the metropolitan area began to sing a newly arranged version of the *Prayer of St. Francis* by Ralph Hunter. October 4 is the feast day of St. Francis of Assisi.

"Lord make me an instrument of Thy peace," the choir sang, as the Pope was being vested for the votive mass for peace.

Although the Pontiff was the only celebrant of the low mass, he was assisted by seven servers and two masters of ceremony who had three aides.

The servers were Monsignor James F. Rigney, bookbearer; Monsignor Thomas J. Kelly, crosier bearer; Monsignor Thomas F. Heneghan, acolyte; Monsignor John J. Snyder, acolyte; Monsignor John P. Sullivan, miterbearer; John A. Coleman, a lay papal chamberlain, who was candlebearer, and Monsignor Mario Nasalli Rocca of the Vatican, who bore the pitcher and basin.

The masters of ceremony were Monsignor Patrick V. Ahern, secretary to Cardinal Spellman and Monsignor Francis X. Duffy, the director of St. Patrick's Information Center.

The Pope wore white vestments, including a cassock, a close-fitting garment with long sleeves; an amice, a white linen collar with a cross embroidered at the center; an alb, a long white linen garment worn over the cassock; a stole, worn around the neck like a scarf; a cincture, a white cord tied about the waist to secure the alb and stole; a chasuble, a poncholike outer vestment made of silk, adorned with crosses and other symbols; a maniple, a silk piece worn over the left forearm that matches the chasuble; a ring; a pectoral cross; a zucchetto, and from time to time a miter, or tall crown.

The Pontiff celebrated the mass in Latin, but the congregation, reading from booklets containing the responses and the four hymns sung, responded in English. He delivered his sermon or homily in English.

"Brothers and sons of New York," he began, "brothers and sons of the United Nations and of all America, all of you who have assembled here from every part of the world, we greet you and we bless you!"

In hesitant, accented English, the Pope spoke of his visit: "This is the day which we have desired for centuries! The day which, for the first time, sees the Pope setting foot on this young and glorious continent!"

In his sermon, the Pope took cognizance of the presence of non-Catholics, such as Dr. Norman Vincent Peale, president of the Protestant Council of New York; Bishop Horace B. Donegan, head of the Episcopal Diocese of New York; Rabbi Simon Greenberg, vice-chancellor of the Jewish Theological Seminary, and Archbishop Iakovos, primate of the Greek Orthodox Church.

The Pope extended his greeting to "those Christian brothers here present, separated from us, yet united with us by baptism and by belief in the Lord Jesus" and to those "who follow other religious beliefs, and who in good conscience intend to seek and honor Almighty God, the Lord of heaven and earth; among whom the descendants of Abraham have our particular consideration."

The principal theme, as it was throughout the day, was peace for mankind. "You must love peace"—"You must serve the cause of peace"—"Peace must be based on moral and religious principles, which will make it sincere and stable," the Pontiff told the hushed assemblage.

"Truly, verily, peace be to you!"

Because of the importance of the United Nations in the Pope's visit portions of the Prayer of the Faithful were recited in the five languages of the United Nations by five lectors, as well as in Latin by Pope Paul.

The Pope began: "Let us pray: Brethren, in this prayer of the people of God, which we are about to offer in common, let each not pray for his own needs, but let us together beseech Christ the Lord for peace for the whole world."

Frank Aiken, Minister for External Affairs of Ireland, recited in English: "That God may continue to guide our church in a ceaseless search for ways to bring the 'peace which the world cannot give' to men who recognize that they are brothers."

Arsene Assouan Usher, Ambassador Extraordinary and Plenipotentiary of the Ivory Coast, spoke the next portion in French: "That God may grant this peace to all peoples and instill trust in place of fear in the community of nations."

In Spanish, Dr. Victor Andres Belaunde, Ambassador Extraordinary and Plenipotentiary of Peru, said: "That God may grant to the officials of all governments wisdom in knowing, courage in accomplishing, and dedication in fulfilling the responsibilities of their office."

Shue mei-Sheng, Counselor at the Mission of the Republic of China to the United Nations, recited in Chinese: "That God may awaken the sympathy of every human heart for those whose hunger and nakedness and exile are the result of armed conflict."

In Russian, Constantine Mertvagos, translator on the staff of the United Nations Secretariat, said: "That God may inspire wise leaders to use the growing mastery of nature to provide the necessities of life and a decent measure of comfort for all men."

At the end of each lector's recital the congregation recited in English: "Grant this, O Lord, we humbly pray."

The Pope, in Latin, concluded the prayer: "O God, our refuge and our strength and source of all goodness, hear the holy prayers of your church and grant that we may fully obtain what we have asked for in faith; through Christ Our Lord."

In English, the throng replied: "Amen."

At the beginning of the Offertory, twelve children, representing the continents, went in procession to the altar and presented to the Pope the water and wine used in the service, the paten on which the consecrated bread in the eucharist was placed, the ciborium containing the host, two candles, a symbolic gold-and-silver loaf of bread, a small wine cask and a small gold wine cask, a gilded olive branch and a wooden dove painted silver.

The only North American was John Nardoza, eleven years old, of Queens, whose name was drawn from a hat at St. Nicholas of Tolentine School.

His father, John A. Nardoza, forty-four, was one of the policemen stationed on the cinder track facing the crowd and he was the only policeman given permission to turn and watch the twelve communicants.

During the canon of the mass—consisting of the consecration of the bread and wine and the taking of communion—the vast stadium was stilled. Only a rhythmic beat could be heard over the public-address system. One spectator said it must have been the sound of the Pope's heart coming through the microphone he wore during the service.

At the end of the mass, which was telecast throughout the United States and sent by Early Bird satellite to Europe, the Pope blessed a cornerstone for a projected new seminary in Yonkers. He also blessed two fragments of ornately carved marble, excavated from St. Peter's Basilica in Rome, that will be part of the cornerstone.

In his sermon, the Pontiff declared, "You can see in this cornerstone an eloquent symbol of the faith and love which unite the Catholics of New York to the Church of Rome."

After the blessing, the night was filled with the rousing strains of Bach's harmonization of "Now Thank We All Our God," written for the German Lutheran Church in the first half of the seventeenth century.

As the Pope retraced his steps along the red carpet to his automobile, the choir chanted *Christus Vincit* (Christ Con-

37

quers), a set of acclamations dating back to the eighth century when they were sung in praise of emperors, popes and monarchs about to be crowned.

"Hear us, O Christ, long life to Paul our Holy Father and Universal Pope," they chanted in Latin. "Saviour of the world come to his aid."

They also sang *Oremus Pro Pontifice,* the classic liturgical prayer for the Pope that was given a new setting for the occasion that was described by one musician as a "modern Latin motet."

As he neared the car, thousands of voices erupted in unrestrained praise for the waving, smiling Pontiff, who shook hands with people in aisle seats.

"Long live the Pope, long live the Pope, long live the Pope," the throng shouted. *"Viva Il Papa, viva il Papa, viva il Papa."*

At 10:05, as the car left the stadium, the tumult subsided, and the organ, choir and brass ensemble struck up the national anthem.

At the Fair: "Goodbye, Goodbye."

By Philip Benjamin

Toward the end of the long day in New York City Pope Paul VI stood in a darkened gallery and gazed at Michelangelo's *Pietà,* the dead Jesus in the arms of Mary.

This was at the World's Fair, and the Pope was only minutes away from boarding his plane for the flight back to Rome. He stood stockstill for nearly a minute; his lips moved in prayer; then he crossed himself, left the gallery, mounted to a balcony and said, in English, "Goodbye, goodbye." On the second "goodbye" he laughed a small, warm laugh and the crowd outside roared its approval, cheered, applauded and shouted *"Viva Il Papa!"*

The Pope had arrived at the World's Fair at 10:25 P.M. through Gate Number 2, where a Catholic high-school band played him in. As the Pope's motorcade passed the Unisphere, fireworks burst into the sky and the bells of the Vatican Pavilion began to peal.

At 10:29 the Pope—accompanied by Cardinal Spellman, five other cardinals and four American archbishops—arrived at the Pavilion, where perhaps ten thousand persons were waiting.

Many of them had begun arriving six hours earlier. Fathers held their children aloft so they could glimpse the Pope, and so that the Pope perhaps could glimpse them. There were great cheers and shouts.

The Pope left his car and walked along a red carpet to the pavilion's entrance, where he was met by Robert Moses, president of the Fair. Nineteen pavilion hostesses in cardinal red were lined up to receive the Pope.

Behind the Pope rose the varicolored tower of the New York State Pavilion. Another touch of color came from the lavender sign of the "Bourbon Street" night club across the way. The Pope's hands fluttered in his characteristic gesture of greeting as he made his way past the crowd and in the face of a chill wind to the pavilion entrance.

The Pope, his entourage and at least fifteen plainclothes detectives moved into the darkened gallery where the *Pietà* is on display behind glass in a setting of blue and green light. The setting was conceived by the theatrical designer Jo Mielziner. Behind him a TV camera bearing the papal coat-of-arms recorded the Pope's reverent pause.

After moving out of the gallery the Pope ascended the staircase to the Chapel of the Good Shepherd; he knelt at a priedieu and, as he had done all day long, he gave his blessing to the assembly "in the name of the Father, and of the Son, and of the Holy Spirit."

He went then to a balcony on the second floor, where he said another prayer. It was then he raised his arms and said, "Goodbye, goodbye." As he descended the staircase, people tried to touch him. Three children, victims of cerebral palsy, caught his attention and he went to them, placed his hands on them and blessed them.

The Pope did not see a mosaic portrait of himself, but he did pause, with Cardinal Spellman, at the main-floor display of his jewel-encrusted gold-and-silver coronation tiara, which he gave to the American people in thanks for American aid to the poor and needy of the world.

The Pope was about the twenty-five-millionth person to visit the Vatican Pavilion, which is second only to the General Motors Futurama in popularity. The Pope's visit lasted twelve minutes; to more cheers and more cries of *"Viva Il Papa!"* he left the pavilion and the Fair, motored to Kennedy International Airport and departed for Rome.

Afterward, at a news conference in the St. Peter's crypt area of the pavilion, Monsignor John J. Gorman, director of the pavilion, said that Pope Paul had made little or no comment on the pavilion. Earlier, however, the Vatican press office had released a statement by the Pope in which he said, in part, "We congratulate our brother, Cardinal Spellman, and all those who have collaborated to produce this wonderful and prayerful result. . . . As we gazed on this moving masterpiece [the *Pietà*], we could not but think of the religious convictions which moved the young Michelangelo to such heights and to such a magnificent result."

Until the Pope left the pavilion, the police had held the crowds in and around it. As they streamed out of and away from the building, many persons wiped their eyes. One woman said to her husband: "I don't know about you, but my knees are weak."

The Return to Rome

By John Cogley

The Pope and his official party arrived at John F. Kennedy airport only a half hour after the scheduled time of departure. In view of the crowds, the number of activities scheduled during the long day, and the distances between the places visited, the delay was understandable. It was in fact much shorter than most of the reporters had anticipated.

TWA was much more security-conscious than Alitalia, the airline he had used for the trip to New York. The reporters and priests returning to Rome with the papal party were required to be at the airport hours before take-off. Baggage was carefully inspected and every precaution as to the identity of passengers taken.

The reporters traveling with the Pope saw the closing events of his stay in New York by color television provided by TWA. The mass at Yankee Stadium was particularly beautiful in the exaggerated tones of the color TV screen. By the time the Pope left the World's Fair Vatican Pavilion, the press people were beginning to board the plane for the trip back to Rome.

Those who had left Rome in the early morning of the same calendar day were utterly exhausted. Most looked considerably more the worse for wear than the man who had been under the merciless eye of television cameras constantly from the time he set foot on American soil.

The reporters were confined to their cabin quarters and missed the entry of the Pope and his party. No one was even sure they had come aboard until engines started to purr. At 11:30 P.M. the plane ascended.

Then there was silence. Conversations softened and finally disappeared altogether as the plane started its journey across the ocean. Sometime during the night, the hostesses began to serve beef steak. A few passengers managed to revive long enough to eat. But all the noise and confusion and expectation of the morning Alitalia trip were notably missing on the return flight.

Later it was announced that Paul VI had retired soon after the plane took off and had slept for about two and a half hours. The dignified cardinals and bishops in attendance, sleepy themselves after trailing after their leader throughout the long day, were blessedly free of prying photographers. But it would not be difficult to imagine the scene in the first-class cabin where elderly churchmen in the comparatively cramped quarters of even first-class accommodations fell into fitful slumber.

Then in the temporal no-mans-land of jet travel, it was suddenly morning though it should have still been night. The girls on duty were serving untimely breakfasts. From time to time a bleary-eyed cardinal appeared in the coach section, shaving kit in hand. The bathroom resources of the first-class section were clearly overtaxed. Cardinal Agaganian, the Dean of the Sacred College, stood patiently in line waiting his turn in the little room. Cardinal Rugambwa, the princely black African, appeared among the newsmen and stopped to chat with a few he knows personally.

There was a sudden commotion when the Pope appeared. Again he walked from seat to seat. Again he distributed the Morial Medal to those who had not already received one and this time added a beautifully turned out souvenir booklet with reproductions of the Vatican postage stamps which had been issued to mark the historic visit.

The passengers congratulated the Pontiff on the success of his mission. He smiled but said little. A few reporters asked questions, but he avoided direct replies with the skill born of years in the Vatican State Department.

The Pontiff had deeper circles under his eyes, his exhaustion though did not appear to be extreme. His disposition appeared to be altogether unaffected. He was just as gentle of manner as he had been thirty-six hours earlier when he appeared to be so fresh and ready for the long day.

He moved slowly through the cabin, missing no one. Meanwhile the photographers clicked, clicked, clicked with that unbending zeal that is characteristic of the profession. But something of the restless enthusiasm of the previous morning had been tamed by the passing of the long hours.

During the night the Pope had sent a message of gratitude to President Lyndon Johnson for the hospitality he had received in the United States. President De Gaulle and Premier De Valera of Ireland had sent greetings to him as the plane passed over their countries.

Finally, some two hours after the Pontiff's last visit to the journalists who had traveled with him, the plane put down in Rome.

There was a crowd waiting at the airport. Paul VI greeted them briefly. He then went directly to St. Peter's, past more cheering street crowds. At St. Peter's, he reported on his trip and appeal for world peace to the bishops of the Vatican Council.

This was the final act in the drama. With the applause of his Bishops ringing in his ears, Paul VI returned to the papal apartments, finally able, one hopes, to sleep the sleep of the just.

From Sleaziest Slum to Sleekest Luxury

By Murray Schumach

Wherever the Pope turned, stopped, prayed or talked, there were the people of the city.

For thirteen hours, almost four million New Yorkers spread themselves along twenty-four miles of street and highway. They lined streets and peered down from skyscrapers. They joined him in church, in stadium and at World's Fair. They brought their children and their grandchildren; their banners and prayers.

For New York, there was a curious feeling of orderliness and restraint. It seemed incredible that so vast a throng, scattered over such varied environments, from sleaziest slum to sleekest luxury, could be so uniformly disciplined.

Most of the day it was as though the millions who had come to see the Pope allowed his gentle smile to curb extravagant cheers and the limp wave of his hand to enjoin excesses in adulation. Always, no matter how closely packed the admiring throng, it maintained the quality of goodwill that reflected the Pope's theme of peace before the United Nations.

There were moments in the day when the emotions broke through the restraints—in front of St. Patrick's, at the Stadium, and at the World's Fair—but always it was brought under control.

Near noon, across the street from St. Patrick's Cathedral, the crowd on Fifth Avenue was packed behind barricade and police lines from the middle of the street, back on the sidewalk, almost to the skyscraper walls of Rockefeller Center.

Down the avenue, behind motorcycles and open cars filled with security men, came the bubble-top limousine, preceded by a growing roar as thousands of spectators spotted the Pope's scarlet robe and white skullcap. Bells began to toll and the crowd edged forward as the Pontiff mounted the steps toward the huge bronze doors, the organ pealing the Papal March and *Tu Es Petrus* (Thou Art Peter). Slowly the barricades began to give way. The police pressed back. Suddenly the crowd caught itself, subsided.

The muted behavior of the crowds during the visit was particularly manifest in the evening, when the Pope said a low mass for peace at the Yankee Stadium. Here, as some ninety thousand persons poured out of subway and elevated, filling the sidewalks around the ball park, they walked shoulder to shoulder. But they showed the decorum of churchgoers as they tried not to jostle one another, excused themselves if they trod on another's feet. Said a police captain: "This is certainly not a raucous crowd."

And when an elderly woman arrived from Morristown, New Jersey, without a ticket, a police lieutenant gave her his own.

At some points along the route, spectators expressed some disappointment that the Pope's car was moving too quickly. This happened along Queens Boulevard, parts of Third Avenue and in Harlem. Most of those complaining were women. Typical of their comments were: "I think it's a shame, after we waited so long"; "That wasn't right what he did"; "I'm grabbing the subway downtown. Maybe I can get a better look where he can't go so fast."

But much more often, spectators expressed pleasure. One woman, after seeing the Pope, was unable to contain herself when she reached a subway station and stopped to give a subway guard a detailed account.

There seemed little disagreement among the hundreds of thousands of children as they waved little papal flags, carried banners of their schools. Generally, however, they became so excited they forgot the advice of teachers who had told them they must genuflect when they saw the Pope. It was for the children that the Pope seemed to beam most broadly: a sort of reward for the chants they had improvised before his arrival— "We want the Pope" and "We want Paul."

On one occasion, the Pope may have heard one of these chants. For a group of youngsters took it up while he was in the Chancery, behind St. Patrick's Cathedral, with Cardinal Spellman. However, they quickly ended their happy game when a voice on a loudspeaker urged them to do so.

The crowds around the Waldorf-Astoria, where the Pope conferred with President Johnson, were an extraordinary lesson in patience, in a neighborhood where people are quick, even for New Yorkers, to complain about delays.

The phenomenon of New York behavior was summed up by a schoolteacher whose students were models for the day.

"Why shouldn't everyone be well behaved today," she asked.

"How often does one get to see the Pope in New York?"

Here and there, there was also a note of unworldliness, and it came from the faces of the nuns. Often, as the Pope passed, they wept as they smiled, remaining motionless for a second or two after the Pontiff had passed. The schoolchildren often seemed to sense this special emotion and waited for the nuns to recover.

One nun, after herding parochial-school girls behind a wooden barricade, spotted the letters "DD" on the color of a police uniform. She asked the husky wearer if this meant "Doctor of Divinity." He curbed a grin as he replied: "No, Sister, Detective Division."

In the Streets of Harlem

By Theodore Jones

Mrs. Julia Rivers wrapped her black leather coat tightly about her and leaned against the wooden police barrier for a better look at the large clock above the northeast corner of 125th Street and Seventh Avenue. It was 10:30 A.M. in Harlem.

"Pretty long wait for a historic moment," she said to no one in particular, but in a voice loud enough to be heard by the Harlem residents who stood in uneven lines behind her. They murmured agreement.

"You're not Catholic, are you," whispered a young woman with a knowing smile.

"No, darling," Mrs. Rivers replied quickly, "I'm Methodist myself but I've been standing here for two hours in the cold just like the Catholics. There's no particular reason to be Catholic to see the Pope, is there?"

The young lady's reply was drowned out by a laugh from the crowd which waited patiently to get a glance of Pope Paul VI at Harlem's busiest intersection.

By 11 A.M., there was a festive air in the crowd of some five thousand adults and parochial-school children who stood five feet deep along 125th Street from Third to Seventh Avenue and along the streets south to 110th Street and Central Park.

The central Harlem community of 232,000 persons is about 95 per cent Protestant, mostly southern Baptist and African Methodist. It has some four hundred churches that range from

45

store-front operations with small memberships to large, luxurious edifices with congregations exceeding four thousand persons.

Also thriving in the community are separatist contingents of Black Jews and Black Muslims, and numerous black nationalist groups, whose sidewalk oratory is stronger than their membership.

Why was the Pope looped through one of the world's most dismal slums?

He wanted it. "If we didn't show him Harlem, we truthfully would not be showing him some of the significant areas of New York," Monsignor T. J. Flynn, director of the bureau of information of the Archdiocese of New York, had explained.

The crowd who came to see the Pope reflected the dominant religious and secular beliefs in the community, although there were a number of large contingents from Catholic schools and parishes in Harlem.

Weaving in and out of the large throng were black nationalists who came to see "what all the fuss was about"; Black Muslims selling copies of *Muhammad Speaks,* the weekly newspaper of the black supremist sect, and Negro and white schoolchildren who raced about waving blue banners proclaiming, "The Pope and Peace."

"Hope we'll be able to see him," remarked an elderly man to a woman next to him. "Here the man comes talking peace and we got so many policemen here that it looks like a military camp."

At 11:20, the Pope's motorcade reached the intersection, turned onto Seventh Avenue and moved swiftly toward Central Park. Cheers and shouts of "God bless the Pope" went up but there were also disappointed cries of "Where is he?" and "What car is he in?"

Many who had stood for several hours failed to see the Pontiff because of the fast-moving motorcade.

"He probably saw more of us than we did of him," remarked Mrs. Evelyn Sears, a young Catholic housewife who had deserted her television set for a personal view. "I sort of missed out but I felt his presence, and so did Harlem."

But it was also in Harlem that Pope Paul VI's motorcade made an unscheduled stop at Lexington Avenue and 125th Street. The brief halt came in front of students from Rice High School, a Roman Catholic school at 124th Street and Lenox Avenue. The Pontiff quickly blessed them from his car and handed one a personally signed message in a sealed envelope.

The Pontiff's note was in answer to an invitation he had received from the interracial student body to visit the twenty-seven-year-old high school during his day in New York. It read:

> *To the students of Rice High School: We received your kind invitation and, during our mission of world peace to the United Nations, we are very happy to see you and to bless you. You are very dear to our heart, and we pray for you that God may give you all the graces you need to be exemplary citizens of your great country.*
>
> *We ask you to pray for us, for Holy Mother Church, for the Vatican Council, and for peace and justice between all the races of mankind. In return, we lovingly bless you, your parents and families, your teachers and your friends.*

The message was signed with the date of the papal visit and the Pope's signature, "Paulis PP. VI."

The Reverend Henry A. Otto, subsuperior of the school, said later no one at Rice had been told that the Pope would stop during his morning motorcade.

"We were flabbergasted," he said with a broad smile.

A Day To Live For

By Philip H. Dougherty

At 5:20 A.M., when Pope Paul VI's DC–8 jet was 2,377 miles from New York, the alarm clock went off in the neat green Colonial home at 94 Ballard Drive, West Hartford, Connecticut. The bell began the day for the family of Richard H. Ware. It would be a long day, an exciting day, an unforgettable day.

While the head of the house went off to sell business equipment in Syracuse, his wife, Constance, the holder of a single ticket to Yankee Stadium, and their three young boys were among the thousands of Roman Catholic out-of-towners who hurried to join New Yorkers along the route of the papal motorcade.

Their reason was probably the same as most. Mrs. Ware voiced it right after the Pope's car, flags whipping in the breeze, drove past their vantage point on Queens Boulevard in Forest Hills, Queens.

Tall, handsome Connie Ware leaned over to Philip, six years

47

old, her youngest, to say, "Many people live and die without ever seeing the Pope."

After the Pope had been seen and cheered, Mrs. Ware drove the youngsters out to her parents' home in Rockville Centre, Long Island, watched him on television and then came back to the city by herself for the mass at the stadium.

The family—the other boys are Stephen, ten, and Bobby, nine—left the house and Duchess, their dog, at 6:30. It was a breezy 50 degrees and still dark. All wore heavy winter jackets. Stephen ("the Irish spelling") wore a yellow "Good Guys" sweatshirt under his.

Two hours later they parked their blue Dodge Lancer on Burns Street in Forest Hills, just two blocks from Queens Boulevard. There was plenty of time for hot chocolate in a jam-packed luncheonette at the corner of Ascan Avenue and the boulevard. Bobby, the energetic second son, spilled his all over the table. "Just like home," the mother said.

The four Wares were behind the ropes on the traffic island between 73d Road and 73d Drive by 9:30. It was clear and cold. Behind them on the awning of Ristorante Italia a banner proclaiming "Viva Il Papa" fluttered. Across the street six terraces on a recently completed fourteen-story apartment house were crowded with nuns.

A block west the sixth, seventh and eighth grades of Our Lady Queen of Martyrs School stood as they had been since 8:30 holding the tiny papal and American flags that had been distributed by their fluttery nuns.

A block east the 124-man band of St. Aloysius School, Ridgewood, was playing Irish airs and nearby were ninety-four parochial-school youngsters and four nuns who had left Dayton, Ohio, at 8 P.M. the previous day for a one-day visit. One carried a sign with bright purple letters: "Welcome Pope Paul."

At 9:45 Mrs. Philomena Turturo of the Bronx, seventy-six, sat down next to Mrs. Ware on a folding chair supplied by her son-in-law as Patrolman Ernest Pasqualini of the 103d Precinct, on duty since 6 A.M., commented on the weather: "Not too bad, only the wind."

"Just leaving the airport," announced Dawson Anderson, a husky man standing nearby with a transistor radio pressed to his ear. The only traffic consisted of police cars, marked and unmarked. Each got a cheer from the growing crowd, three deep along that part of the route.

"Just left the airport," a sergeant told Patrolman Pasqualini at 10 o'clock. Young Philip gave a yawn. Two minutes later he and his brother scooted over to a Hungarian pastry shop and returned with huge chocolate-chip cookies. While they were gone, their mother, stamping her feet in the cold, adjusted her little camera.

A gust of wind blew off a policeman's hat. Everyone cheered. A man went by selling papal pennants and pins. "Business is pretty good," he said.

By 10:25 Bobby was perched like a lookout on the base of a lamppost. Blocks away, near Union Turnpike, a red light was flashing.

"Here he comes," the boy shouted.

"Look at all the helicopters," Stephen yelled as about ten copters forming the papal air cover swept in above the motorcade. Everyone pushed forward to the curb's edge.

Red lights flashing, they came: a police car, a motorcycle, another police car, a vanload of policemen, three more police cars, a wedge of roaring motorcycles, and then a big black limousine with flags flying from its fenders—the Pope.

"Yay!" shouted the three Ware brothers, clapping furiously. Then he was gone. The man behind the boys dropped his camera. "I didn't get him," he sobbed. "I got the wrong car."

"I got a good picture of the back of his head," said Mrs. Ware.

"The first Pope to visit American soil," proclaimed Bobby solemnly.

By 10:34 the last of the motorcade was out of sight and the Wares started back to their car as the St. Aloysius band, playing an off-tune "Tea for Two," marched back to buses.

The Wares had seen the Pope. The Pope, however, had been looking the other way. The boys were at the home of their grandparents, the Charles K. Everetts, before the Pope reached St. Patrick's Cathedral.

Mrs. Ware took the Long Island's 4:22 out of Rockville Center to return alone to the city. After a walk on Fifth Avenue and a visit to St. Patrick's she took the crowded Independent subway to Yankee Stadium.

Most parishes in this area had drawings for the tickets they were allotted. In other cities, where fewer tickets were received, it was first come, first served at the diocesan offices. Mrs. Ware, one of five hundred requesting tickets at the Hartford chancery, said she sent her letter a week ahead of time to the Archbishop's secretary, who knew her as the chairman of a theater benefit that had raised $15,000 for a Catholic charity. She got her ticket

49

—Section 20, Row E, Seat 17, just nine rows from the top of the stadium behind third base.

She sat next to Mother Stanislas of the Little Sisters of the Poor from New Haven, whose field glasses she shared, in the same row with a fellow parishioner from St. Thomas the Apostle Church in West Hartford.

Mrs. Ware was in her seat, her black lace mantilla with its white trim covering her head, an hour and a quarter before the Pope arrived. The time went quickly though as she and the nuns beside her tried to spot dignitaries arriving in the infield below them.

As sharp-eyed as her son Bobby, she was the first to see the flashing red lights of the Pope's motorcade over the top of the bleachers coming west on 161st Street. She stood with the rest and clapped and clapped when the Pope entered the stadium and again when he left. Most of the remaining ninety minutes were spent in rapt devotion.

During the inching forty-five-minute return with the crowd to the subway station, she was misty-eyed. "The most moving experience," she said to a priest from Upper New York, New Jersey, next to her. "It was fantastic. Corporate worship with ninety thousand people."

Later, over a hamburger while waiting for the 11:58 to Rockville Centre, she said, "I'd get up at five-twenty tomorrow and do it all over again."

A Day for Children

By Richard J. H. Johnston

Pope Paul VI raised his hand in blessing as he faced the throng in Fifth Avenue from the steps of St. Patrick's Cathedral.

"Look straight at him, Johnny," said a man holding a small, pale boy high on his shoulders.

"He sees me, he sees me, Daddy," cried the child.

The man lowered the boy gently to the sidewalk, then he bent to adjust the braces on each of the boy's thin legs.

"Now let's go and say a prayer," the father said.

For both father and son it appeared to be a moment of transcendent hope as they made their way slowly away from the throng.

Throughout the day the Pope and the children seemed to reach out across the adult world of trouble and fear to each other. The Pontiff's eyes appeared to glow each time his gaze caught here a lone child waving and smiling and there an orderly rank of parochial-school children greeting him with disciplined decorum.

Monsignor Raymond P. Rigney, Superintendent of Schools for the Archdiocese of New York, said that 700,000 parochial-school children in New York, New Jersey and Connecticut had been given a holiday so they could see the Pope.

They came by bus, train, car and on foot to line the Pope's route from Kennedy International Airport to St. Patrick's Cathedral. And as he passed, giving his greeting and blessing, they waved their school banners high and cheered.

At the Manhattan end of the Queensborough Bridge the military band from St. Francis Xavier High School burst into a martial tune as the Pope's car approached.

Farther along the route several boys held aloft handmade signs on broomsticks.

"Prayer," "Faith," "Kindness," the signs read.

Among the children were little detached knots of boys and girls apparently not associated with any official greeting.

The city's Department of Education had issued no orders excusing public-school children for the day. But principals were told they might "exercise discretion."

The parochial-school groups began to gather in many places at least two hours before the Pope's arrival.

Chilled by a biting wind that made the mid-forty-degree temperatures seem colder, spirits flagged from time to time.

"He isn't coming," said a small boy, sobbing.

"He is, too; he's the Pope, isn't he?" his sister said.

Another little boy began to sob after the Pontiff had gone by.

"What's wrong, Peter?" asked his teacher.

"I waved so much I forgot to take his picture," replied the boy.

Along Queens Boulevard two boys pedaled their bikes furiously to keep abreast of the Pope's open limousine. They held him in close view for more than three blocks.

All along the route children waved small papal flags or held aloft rosary beads and religious medals in the hope of having them blessed.

As the motorcade entered Central Park, on the way to St. Patrick's, 650 boys and girls from Albertus Magnus High School in Bardonia, New York, stood in orderly ranks in the bright sunlight. At a signal from their supervisor, Sister Noela Miriam, they raised their voices in a resounding cheer.

At a curve in Central Park, a small boy jumped up and down, his eyes bright with wonder.

"I saw him, I saw him, he was all in white!" he cried to no one in particular, but obviously to the world in general.

A uniformed fourteen-year-old parochial-school girl, observed somberly: "I hope this does some good at the United Nations."

The moment when Pope Paul VI and the children came closest together occurred at the United Nations. There a group representing many nations, the sons and daughters of U.N. ambassadors, presented him with a bouquet of roses on behalf of the United Nations Children's Fund. The gesture focused attention on the Vatican's firm support of the fund.

The presentation was made by Amer, the nine-year-old son of Soubhi J. Khanachet, a representative of Kuwait to the United Nations. The bouquet of yellow tea roses had been plucked from the U.N. garden.

Pope Paul thanked the children on behalf of himself and his church and added: "I will pray for you."

A Transfixed City

By Bernard Weinraub

For thirteen hours New York was gripped by a drama whose giant audience left parts of the city numb and virtually paralyzed.

It was, in a sense, as if Fifth, Park and Lenox Avenues and Queens Boulevard had stopped breathing as the frail visitor moved about.

Stores were boarded up and some even closed in the morning, appointments were canceled, traffic was rerouted, shoppers were rare and office work was, for many, impossible.

"How can we work?" asked Marianne Micros, a pretty, dark-haired receptionist at *Look* magazine on 488 Madison Avenue, across the street from Cardinal Spellman's residence. "Everyone's trying to sneak off to the windows to have a peek."

On Wall Street, trading activity on the New York Stock Exchange slowed to about 5.6 million shares from about 7.5 million on the previous Friday. In Harlem, men and women rushed out of furniture and department stores on 125th Street as soon as the roar of police motorcycles leading Pope Paul VI's entourage were heard. And in midtown, in shops and department stores, there were far more police and security guards than customers before noon.

"There might as well have been a blizzard outside for all the business we did," a spokesman for a large Fifth Avenue department store said.

"Up to noon there were no customers in the store, and I mean none."

For the day at least, salesgirls in department stores casually forgot to inventory, paying attention only to tiny transistor radios hidden behind counters and then quietly passing the word, "He's now in Harlem . . . he's now in Central Park."

With numerous business appointments canceled in advertising agencies and publishing houses on Madison and Fifth Avenues, many windows were simply flung open (against police orders) as the morning wore on, and employees left their desks to look outside.

Outside, for the midtown motorist, it was a day of the impossible—impossible to park, impossible to move, impossible to turn on any one of a dozen city streets.

Many motorists heeded Traffic Commissioner Henry A. Barnes's advice and took buses and subways to work. Rush-hour service was in effect all day on all rapid-transit and surface facilities.

Others drove to work—many with their children—at 7 A.M. At that hour, the Van Wyck Expressway and Queens Boulevard were unusually crowded, while an hour later, as police protection tightened, the roads were unusually empty.

In the city, traffic was rerouted an hour and sometimes longer before the Pope passed certain spots: Lenox and Seventh Avenues near 125th Street, Queens Boulevard, the Queensborough Bridge, the Major Deegan Expressway, Grand Central Parkway, the lower Grand Concourse, the Willis Avenue Bridge, River Avenue and 161st Street and parts of Fifth, Madison and Park Avenues.

For the city dweller, carless Fifth and Park Avenues left an unexpected reward. While crowds gathered at one spot along one street to wait for the Pope, one could stroll for three or four or even five blocks in the middle of Park Avenue, empty of traffic and free of noise.

For the driver outside midtown who avoided the Pope's route, there was also an unexpected reward. "Let's have the

Pope here every day," said a cab driver on the upper East Side, parts of which had a remarkably easy flow of traffic.

And for the driver and city dweller and visitor, there was one more unexpected reward. The city's Department of Highways placed a two-thousand-man crew on the streets to make sure there wasn't a single pothole along the Pope's motor route. Commissioner John T. Carroll said his crews had been working a week to repair the roads the Pope traveled.

As visitors flooded the city in the morning, midtown Manhattan appeared to be swept up in a mild and not unexpected frenzy that would end only when the Pope departed.

Wooden boards were placed around the windows of Saks Fifth Avenue, masking from the crowds Louis Feraud's cocktail dresses and a "Seventh Heaven Boutique." The Scribner's bookstore at 597 Fifth Avenue opened at 12:30 P.M., three hours late. Behind the bronze gates of Cartier, Inc., the jewelers at Fifth Avenue and Fifty-second Street, a $100,000 marquise diamond necklace was quietly removed from the window and placed in a vault until Tuesday.

Shortly before noon, when restaurants and sandwich shops usually start filling up, there were empty tables and waiters were standing in doorways. In the Rainbow Room atop Rockefeller Center, at least a half dozen businessmen with binoculars were focusing in on St. Patrick's Cathedral.

In a near-empty Schrafft's, on 51st Street and Madison Avenue just across from Cardinal Spellman's residence, Mrs. Robert F. Kennedy rushed in with a detective and looked toward the counter. "I'm supposed to meet Bobby here, but I guess he's late," she said.

Mrs. Kennedy sat at the counter and ordered a cup of black coffee. "It's so humiliating," she said. "I left all my tickets [for the masses at St. Patrick's Cathedral and at Yankee Stadium] in my other bag. I'll have to explain myself, I suppose."

In a moment, Senator Kennedy entered with an aide. Mrs. Kennedy, leaving her coffee virtually untouched, greeted him and they left quickly for the St. Patrick's mass.

By 1 P.M., with the mass over, the restaurants were packed. "It's like St. Patrick's Day," said Theodore Pilalis, the owner of Teddy's Sandwich Shop on 49 West Fifty-second Street.

Up the street, at the 21 Club, Gary Liptak, a receptionist, remarked: "Oh yes, it really is busier than an average Monday."

By early afternoon, midtown appeared to be returning to

THE DAY'S EVENTS

THE
HISTORIC VISIT
OF
POPE PAUL VI
OCTOBER 4, 1965

I

middle of Madison Avenue from where she could get an unobstructed view of the Pontiff. The two nuns clapped and giggled and jumped up and down when the Pope drove by.

* * *

And people were determined to be polite—or at least to control their tempers.

On Fifth Avenue, in the great crush outside St. Patrick's Cathedral, a neatly dressed man placed his attaché case on the ground beside him. Another man promptly stepped up on it to get a better view.

"Get off it, you ——," the owner started to say. He paused before finishing the word and settled for, "Anyway, get off it." A nearby police officer smiled and said, "You see, it's almost as if they were all in church."

* * *

A schoolgirl at the corner of Third Avenue and 116th Street, along the route the papal motorcade took to the United Nations, patted a familiar mounted policeman's horse and noted: "How clean he is today." The officer smiled down and said, "Yeah, we even brushed his teeth today."

* * *

But not everybody was interested in Pope-watching. One young man in gray flannel and carrying an attaché case was stopped as he scurried across East 61st Street and asked if he intended to see the Pope.

"Pope? I'm more interested in Dow Jones," he replied and hurried off about his business.

* * *

Who's Lieutenant Buckley?

In front of the United Nations another mounted officer stood high in the stirrups, looked over a hedge as the Pope's car swung into view and excitedly shouted to his comrades: "Can you beat that? He's not only riding with Cardinal Spellman but with Lieutenant Buckley too."

* * *

Perspective: Harry Reasoner interrupted a CBS-TV round-table discussion on the Pope's visit to New York to announce that "the jet carrying Walter Cronkite, and also the Pope, is now over Newfoundland."

* * *

a workday tempo. Banks began filling. Shoppers drifted into department stores. Cars returned to Fifth and Park Avenues.

In offices, however, the television set remained as important—perhaps more important—than the typewriter, the adding machine, the telephone.

And at the Magnavox Showcase, 48th Street and Madison Avenue, more than a thousand persons stood before nine television sets to watch the Pope's United Nations speech. At one set, in the middle of the speech, the silence was broken suddenly by a woman who exclaimed loudly: "He looks so tired. I hope he gets some rest. He needs some rest. . . ."

The speech, and all of the Pope's televised activities, were also viewed in hotels—hotels that had filled rapidly over the weekend with many visitors from New England, the Midwest and upper New York.

At the New York Hilton, 95 per cent of the hotel's 2,150 rooms were filled. "We're much busier than usual for this time," observed Paul Filip, the assistant manager. The St. Regis, Gotham, Edison and other hotels also reported "an unprecedented number of reservations."

And at the Concourse Plaza Hotel, near Yankee Stadium, Larry Brownfeld, the assistant manager, said the hotel was almost full.

"It's sort of like the World Series," Mr. Brownfeld said, "except there are more ladies."

"It's Almost As If They Were All in Church"

BY MARTIN ARNOLD

There were many moments of gentleness in a city not known for gentleness.

On Madison Avenue, across the street from Cardinal Spellman's residence, the police had effectively jammed thousands of people behind barricades and few could glimpse the Pope.

Two nuns, one very short, kept trying to push through the crowd so they could see the Pope. Patrolmen, politely but firmly, kept turning them back.

A police sergeant watching the scene finally took each nun by the hand and led her past the wooden barricade into the

II

IV

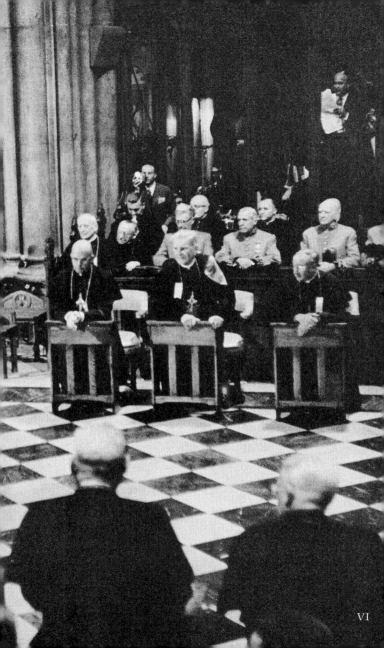

VI

VII

X

XII

XIV

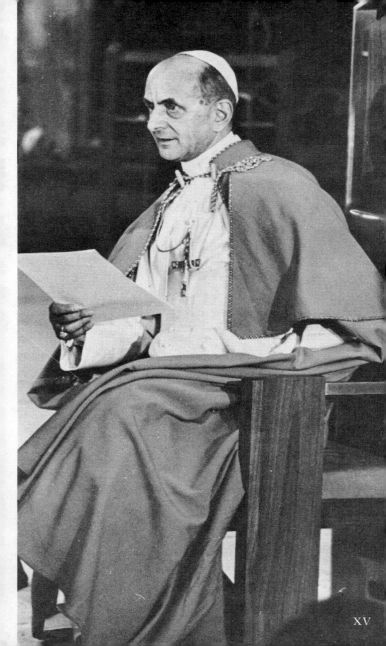

XVIII

XX

XXI

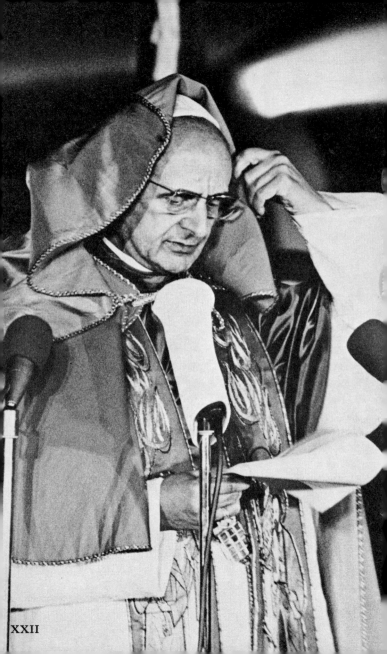

Put handsome policemen beside pretty girls and let them stand together for hours and what happens? They flirt, naturally. So it was. The girls in the crowds whiled away the hours flirting with policemen, leading one ranking officer to comment, "It will be late tonight before many of these boys get home."

* * *

Everyone exchanged gifts. The Pope gave President Johnson a painting by the Italian artist Filocamo entitled *The Resurrected Christ,* and received in return a small gold world globe, two-and-a-half inches in diameter, engraved: "To His Holiness, Pope Paul VI, from Lyndon B. Johnson, President of the United States, October 4, 1965." The President also gave the Pontiff an autographed photograph in a sterling silver frame.

Mrs. Johnson and her daughter, Luci, eighteen, a recent convert to Roman Catholicism, were given religious miniatures by the Pope, and Vice-President Humphrey and Secretary of State Rusk received small contemporary landscapes.

Mayor Wagner gave the Pontiff a solid gold blotter with the seal of the city on one side and that of the Vatican on the other. A gold letter opener was a companion piece.

Cardinal Spellman presented the Pope with a gold medallion commemorating his visit. On one side it bore the image of the Pope and his coat-of-arms. The other side had St. Francis of Assisi's prayer: "Lord, make me an instrument of Thy peace."

* * *

A jewelry store in the immediate vicinity of St. Patrick's Cathedral cleared all the wristwatches and necklaces and rings from its windows so as not to tempt the crowds, and other stores boarded up their windows to prevent anyone from being pushed through them.

* * *

The police managed to keep the souvenir peddlers as far away from St. Patrick's Cathedral as possible. They were pushed all the way back to Sixth Avenue, and some did a brisk business anyhow. Buttons with the Pope's picture on them sold for 50 cents, 75 cents and $1. White pennants proclaiming "Welcome Pope Paul" also sold for $1.

But one vendor said, "Ringo buttons sell better than the Pope's. I thought I'd sell at lot more than I have."

* * *

A Good Humor man wearing a blue knitted cap pushed his cart along Park Avenue and in the chilly weather people hooted his optimism. "If you had hot coffee, then you would do some business," one annoyed woman snapped at him.

* * *

The city was splendid in its uniforms. Eight mobile Red Cross first-aid stations were set up along the twenty-four-mile route traveled by the Pope's motorcade, with uniformed nurses in each.

More than one thousand civil-defense auxiliary police were pressed into service to help the police. And throughout the city, detectives and plainclothesmen, many wearing their uniforms for the first time in years, resembled aging veterans at an American Legion convention. There were uniformed firemen acting as police, and brown-clothed Sanitation Department men giving the city a massive sweep. "The Pope is going to see a clean New York," Deputy Commissioner Jeff Roach said grimly.

* * *

Two girls were walking near St. Patrick's. One, very annoyed, said: "He wanted to be a philosopher. But I asked him, 'How many times have you picked up the Sunday *Times* and read Philosopher Wanted in the want ads?' So he finally got a job. Today was his first day on the job, and I see him standing out here all morning."

* * *

The nuns at Cathedral High School in the Bronx got an emergency call: Ninety thousand copies of the Pope's speech at Yankee Stadium were needed. Working all night, they typed and mimeographed. Not having enough equipment or paper of their own, they ran their own messenger service to other Roman Catholic institutions in the city, which helped produce the copies. The work was done at 2 A.M. and the nuns were able to sleep for several hours before attending five-o'clock mass.

* * *

Earl Blackwell runs Celebrity Service and writes for *Town and Country* magazine. He could have had one of the seats inside St. Patrick's, but decided against it.

"I see the Pope in Rome once a year. I think it's the people who don't go to Rome who should see him," he said.

Mr. Blackwell has had private audiences with Popes Pius XI,

Pius XII, John XXIII and Paul VI, and so he joined a group of watchers in a Fifth Avenue office, where coffee, champagne and little sandwiches were served. A guest said she thought the whole idea was "divine."

* * *

The man in the gray business suit and chauffeur's cap who drove the limousine in which the Pope rode was Neil J. Smith, 48, a husky six-footer. He is the chief chauffeur in New York for the Ford Motor Company, and is known as a "calm, cool and collected" driver. He had previously chauffeured about New York, King Hussein, Prince Bernhard of Belgium and Mrs. John F. Kennedy. In preparation for the Pope's visit, Mr. Smith took several dry runs over the route of the Pope's motorcade, and then pronounced, "I can handle just about anything."

* * *

It was a great day for faces in the crowd, and, therefore, for camera buffs. Bishops and nuns, and even cardinals, carried cameras, but an observer noted that many of the nuns became so joyous when they finally saw the Pope they forgot to snap their pictures.

Two Sisters of Mercy from Notre Dame High School in Trenton, New Jersey, Sister Dennis and Sister Andrew, set some sort of record for length of time peering through opera glasses. They were at it seemingly continuously from 7 A.M. to noon, across the street from St. Patrick's.

Eight Sisters from Philadelphia, in gray gowns and blue cowls, viewed the proceedings very solemnly until a woman standing nearby jabbed her small son in the side and said, "That's the real Pope." The Sisters started to laugh.

* * *

Where there's a will, there's probably a way. One short, slender Italian priest calmly marched toward an entrance of St. Patrick's to hear the Pope offer mass. Asked how he expected to get in without a special pass, he shrugged his shoulders and replied, "I'll sneak in." Result, unknown.

* * *

Office girls who ventured into the streets near St. Patrick's during their lunch hours had an impossible job getting back to work. Overheard time and again was the plea, "But I work just over there," and the answer from a policeman, "Sorry, miss, you'll have to go around the block." The entrances to the Crowell-Collier Publishing Company buildings were blocked by iron fencing and to get through an office worker had to show a uniformed guard a special pass printed for the occasion.

* * *

Throughout the city there was the feeling that everything was geared to the papal visit. Nothing else and no one else seemed to matter, and most people accepted this fact good-naturedly. Perhaps it was best summed up by a police inspector making last-minute arrangements to control the throngs of people waiting outside the Waldorf-Astoria. He said: "His Holiness and the other fellow are meeting here."

That "other fellow" was President Johnson.

* * *

As a final papal salute to the city, the plane carrying Pope Paul VI flew over and up the Hudson River and then down the East River before turning toward Rome. There was a portable television set on the airliner, and the Pope was able to watch his own departure on it.

A Formidable Day for the Police

By Peter Kihss

"Security is not the problem," the Police Commissioner of New York declared as the morning sun lit Kennedy International Airport. "The problem is a great deal of affection, and it's manifestations of that that we have to control."

With that affection moving great crowds to witness the peace mission of Pope Paul VI, New York City's Police Department turned out the greatest force of men in its history—15,000 men. By dint of leapfrog deployment, those 15,000 did the work of 20,000. It was perhaps the department's most formidable day, with President Johnson also in town for his seventeenth presidential visit.

As the Pope was leaving, Commissioner Vincent L. Broderick, lean and serious, said his men's work had been "superb." More than anything else, he credited advance planning by Chief Inspector John F. Shanley and Chief of Staff William J. McQuade. He estimated that their planning had enabled more than 3.8 million persons to see the Pope in generally striking reverence and exemplary order, a contrast to the city's often whooping exuberance.

Once, the tactical patrol force—one hundred specially trained six-footers—had to be rushed in to help other policemen brace wooden barriers holding back enthusiastic noontime throngs outside St. Patrick's Cathedral, where Pope Paul VI finished his twenty-four-mile motorcade.

When the Pontiff's car later began to leave the United Nations, would-be private picture-takers and other onlookers surged around and in front of his car as it unexpectedly backed up. Police motorcyclists roared through to disperse them within forty seconds. That was on United Nations' territory, where one police official stressed that the New York police "do not interfere except to help."

New York's Police Department is largely Catholic—60 per cent of its 26,000 members belong to Holy Name Societies. Commissioner Broderick, now forty-five years old, used to be an altar boy at Our Lady of Esperanza Church on West 156th Street and later was president of Princeton's Catholic Club in his college days.

Riding with the Pope as bodyguard was Chief of Detectives Philip J. Walsh, a bespectacled, tireless and tough policeman. He held a tan briefcase that, he said, contained a portable radio and "some other things." Chief Walsh, forty-six, has attended Our Lady of Perpetual Help Church in Bay Ridge since he was seven. When he reached Kennedy Airport at 6 A.M., it would have been the hour of the earliest mass—but he had attended "quite a few" others in preceding prayerful days.

The first police orders on plans for the visit—T.O.P. 277, for "Temporary Operating Procedures"—had been emblazoned with a shield that carried the triple-tiered papal crown. Later orders directed the men not to let their attention be distracted from their "primary duty of protecting His Holiness."

They had to face the spectators. They were not to remove hats. They were not to take part in religious ceremonies by praying, kneeling or doing anything that might induce reflex actions that could stir up a crowd.

Days off and the start of vacations had been canceled. Some 500 men answered invitations to volunteer to return from vacations. Most of those on duty worked twelve-hour—instead of eight-hour—tours, making them equivalent to a man and a half apiece, at overtime costing the city $1 million in cash.

The ranks were stretched by 300 Port of New York Authority policemen at Kennedy Airport, 800 auxiliary policemen from the Office of Civil Defense and 250 City Housing Authority policemen.

Detectives donned uniforms—often for the first time in years—and Secret Service men helped guard President Johnson. Gray-coated United Nations' security guards joined in the job.

Under William J. Kanz, assistant superintendent of telegraph, the Police Department set up its most elaborate communications network. For the first time it included a new $35,000 headquarters vehicle that was parked outside the United Nations; it had sixteen radio frequencies, a television monitor, four telephones, its own generator and walkie-talkies by the score.

Streets were sealed off to traffic before the Pope's journeys and on key highways, among them Van Wyck Expressway and Queens Boulevard, in both directions. Queensborough Bridge was emptied beforehand. It was a job comparable to a surgeon tying off arteries, a control planned by Assistant Chief Inspector John J. King, commanding the Safety Division, an expert on the city's traffic flow.

Bus lines were rerouted. Nearly one hundred streets had to be kept open for fire engines. Tow trucks helped empty the streets being used, drawing on fleets of the Sanitation and Fire Departments.

Criminal Court cases, including thousands involving traffic summonses, were rescheduled to other days to let policemen defer appearances. Commissioner Broderick, in the midst of the shutdown of six newspapers in labor trouble, broadcast taped appeals for people to stay home, to watch events by television, to travel by public transportation instead of car, to have children wear identification tags in case they became lost. Special telephone services advised truckers on alternate routes.

The night before the Pope's arrival, Commissioner Broderick and Chief Shanley made a last-minute inspection of St. Patrick's Cathedral, before sleeping at the Waldorf-Astoria Hotel. By 6 A.M., their forces were gathering at Kennedy Airport, deploying along the motorcade route, three and a half hours before Pope Paul VI's Alitalia DC–8 came in on schedule.

Only four minutes after the seventeen-car papal motorcade began moving from the airport apron, a quarter mile or so, the cars halted. Motorcycles and a green tactical patrol bus raced up to the Pope's open car.

"The Pope is going to switch cars," a voice announced.

For emergency, a bubble-top limousine had been No. 11 in the motorcade, in case the open papal car, No. 6, suffered a breakdown or the weather turned bad. At that point, chill winds were tearing at the Pontiff's robe, blowing off his broad-brimmed hat.

The plastic-topped limousine is normally used by Mrs. Lyndon B. Johnson, having initially been adapted for Mrs. John F. Kennedy by the Ford Motor Company, which still owns it and also the car originally occupied by the Pope.

The bubble-top limousine's occupants were moved to other cars; the Pope and his party clambered in. The pilgrimage for peace resumed.

Behind ten thousand wooden barricades, the crowds waited. Stakes driven into earth and rigged with long ropes also helped control crowds.

Messages interchanged over the motorcade's radios. Monsignor Pasquale Macchi, the Pope's secretary, riding with him, talked in Italian with Monsignor Paul Marcinkus, of the Vatican Secretariat, who had handled advance plans.

Might the weather moderate to permit changing cars again, perhaps at Queensborough Bridge? Much questioning. Car 240, occupied by Commissioner Broderick, asked Police Headquarters to query the Weather Bureau. No, the forecast saw temperatures of 46 degrees, winds of 10 to 15 miles an hour, gusts up to 30.

Car 179, the Pope's, asked for a check on where Rice High School students might be standing. The word came back—north side of 125th Street between Park and Madison Avenues. The Pope would have a message to hand over; the motorcade should "decelerate," not stop. The police network arranged to have a youthful student with a police escort pick it up.

Another message: The Pope would like to stop at Third Avenue and 68th Street. He did. It was New York Foundling Hospital, and a choir was singing, at one of Cardinal Spellman's favorite charities.

"Inform Cardinal it will be impossible to stop at any other location," the radio came on. "We must positively arrive at the cathedral by a quarter to twelve."

While five police helicopters patrolled overhead and an Emergency Service Division truck carrying oxygen trailed behind, the motorcade rolled through Queens at 16 miles an hour. In Harlem at 11:23 A.M., the radio reported it behind schedule by three and a half minutes. The procession sped up to 20 miles an hour, then reached 23 and 26 in Central Park. Out on Fifth Avenue, it reached St. Patrick's on the scheduled dot.

In Manhattan, security details ordered windows closed at key points and posted guards on Park Avenue and nearby roofs.

For the Pope's United Nations visit, two police launches and a Coast Guard cutter plied the East River, adding to the security patrols. Last fall, a bazooka shell had been fired from the opposite shore toward the world organization's headquarters, cascading into the river in a demonstration by Cuban exiles against Ernesto (Che) Guevara, who had been addressing the General Assembly in behalf of Premier Fidel Castro.

An extra check of Yankee Stadium by the police bomb squad took place during the afternoon, when a telephone caller asserted he had overheard three men talk about an explosive device planted there.

At the World's Fair, the Vatican Pavilion doors were shut

at 4 P.M., six hours before the Pope's scheduled visit, with a security check then getting under way.

Before the Pope boarded a Trans World Airlines aircraft for Rome, the plane was fueled from yellow tank trucks that had been previously checked, and the plane's tanks were then immediately sealed. Baggage underwent police fluoroscoping.

Two suspected pickpockets were arrested during the afternoon in the St. Patrick's Cathedral area, and a third at Yankee Stadium just before Pope Paul VI celebrated his mass for peace. One policeman was treated for a head laceration at Roosevelt Hospital when he fell to the sidewalk in a faint while helping handle the crowd at Fifth Avenue and 53d Street.

The Pilot and the Bible

BY RICHARD WITKIN

For centuries, popes have been figures of tradition, dressed as scores of earlier popes were dressed, moving about on a throne borne by men on foot.

Pope Paul VI, dressed in familiar white skullcap and robes, arrived in the New World in a 550-mile-an-hour jet plane that had made the nonstop 4,300-mile flight from Rome in just under nine hours.

He had flown before, the first pope to do so while holding the papal office. Yet, for the thousands who watched at Kennedy International Airport and the millions who viewed the arrival on television, the sight of the Pope stepping forth from the wing-swept Alitalia jet was still cast in a glow of incongruity.

A similar sight awaited them fourteen hours later when, after his strenuous rounds of the city in his pursuit of peace, the Pope was to board a Trans World Airlines jet for the return flight to Rome.

The captain on the westward Alitalia flight was the same pilot who had flown Pope Paul VI on his trip to the Holy Land in January, 1964, forty-nine-year-old Gianmario Zuccarini. This had been the first time a pope in office had flown.

The plane that brought the Pope from Rome touched down at Kennedy Airport just three minutes before a 9:30 arrival time that had been tentatively established days before.

The pilot had taken a more northerly route than originally planned, to avail himself of lower-than-normal headwinds.

Otherwise, said Captain Zuccarini, who flew Italian fighters during World War II, the flight was smooth and, from an aeronautical viewpoint, uneventful.

"The Pope came to the cockpit at one point and said we must be about two-thirds of the way across the ocean," the Captain said. "He was right."

Air-traffic controllers separated the papal plane from other traffic by larger distances than the one thousand feet (vertically) and three miles (horizontally) that are standard.

The airport's armada of crash equipment was supplemented by extra municipal vehicles. Police helicopters hovered overhead as the plane taxied across the apron.

The captain on the eastward TWA trip was a onetime Presbyterian deacon, fifty-six-year-old Captain George C. Duvall, who headed a crew that included members of three faiths.

When he came to the airport nine hours ahead of the scheduled 11:30 P.M. takeoff to prepare for the flight to Rome, Mr. Duvall had under his arm a huge $100-a-copy book whose publication had led to his assignment to the papal flight.

The train of events that brought Mr. Duvall to the captain's seat for the flight to Rome began more than a decade ago when he was making TWA flights out of Chicago.

"I was an average church layman at the start," recounted the six-foot-five pilot, "just going to church on Sundays. A Revised Standard Version of the Bible had come out and I was having difficulty obtaining copies to give as Christmas presents."

It was while looking for the books that he ran across the Reverend Don Cleveland Norman, then secretary of the Chicago Bible Society.

Mr. Norman helped him find the books he wanted, and this was the beginning of a close association.

Mr. Duvall was subsequently instrumental in having his airline put Bibles aboard all its planes.

And a few years later, Mr. Norman set himself the task of locating the forty-seven original Gutenberg Bibles believed to remain of the almost five hundred printed five centuries ago. No such accounting had been made since the upheaval of World War II.

The pilot mapped an itinerary for his friend, who was able eventually to track down forty-five of the Gutenberg volumes in far corners of the world.

The accounting was made into an illustrated book called

66

The 500th Anniversary Pictorial Census of the Gutenberg Bible, and was priced at $100 a copy.

The next event was a move by Mr. Duvall to obtain funds for Mr. Norman to attend ceremonies marking the restoration of the Gutenberg Museum in Mainz, West Germany. Mr. Duvall prevailed on TWA to purchase six copies.

These were presented to six libraries, one of them the Vatican Library. Mr. Duvall personally made the presentation to the Pope two years ago.

So, when TWA was selected for the return flight of Pope Paul VI, Mr. Duvall was almost the inevitable choice to command the crew.

When he left his Greenwich, Connecticut home at noon the day of the flight, Mr. Duvall carried with him another copy of the book. He hoped to have it autographed by the Pope sometime during the journey.

"I'm honored, deeply honored," the pilot said of his selection for the flight. "But I doubt that I, as a former deacon in the Presbyterian church, would have been chosen for this honor five years ago.

"I think," he added, "this shows some of the great ecumenical progress that has been made at the Vatican Council in Rome."

Cardinal Spellman's Great Day

By Eric Pace

It was an exhausting but exhilarating day for the Pope's host, Francis Cardinal Spellman, the sixth Archbishop of New York. The Pontiff embraced the Cardinal a moment after he stepped from his jetliner at Kennedy Airport, and later greeted him formally before the altar of St. Patrick's Cathedral as "our beloved son."

As the Pontiff waved to the multitudes on his route to the cathedral, Cardinal Spellman was seated beside him in the limousine, wearing a red-trimmed black cassock and red silk sash. Millions saw him, his round, smiling face contrasting with the Pope's sharper features, his close-cut white hair peeping from under his cardinal's red "zucchetto," or skullcap.

"This is His Eminence's great day," said one monsignor on the Cardinal's own staff. It was the high point of his nineteen years as Cardinal, and of a career in the church that began in 1916, when Francis Joseph Spellman, a Massachusetts-born Fordham graduate, was ordained at St. Apollinaris' Church in Rome.

After a succession of administrative and editorial posts, Father Spellman was named Auxiliary Bishop of Boston in 1932 and Archbishop of New York in 1939, a post so prestigious that the Archbishop's Chancery has been called "the Powerhouse."

The Cardinal had long known Giovanni Battista Montini. He had served as attaché in the Vatican Secretariat of State and translator of papal broadcasts from 1925 to 1932, the year Pope Pius XI named the future Pope Paul VI to a clerkship at the Secretariat. When Father Montini visited the United States twice before becoming Pope, Cardinal Spellman received him at his gray neo-Gothic residence on Madison Avenue, adjoining the cathedral.

Cardinal Spellman had overseen careful preparations for the papal visit. The papal arms were hung over the cathedral's portal and on the Cardinal's own throne within. Yellow marigolds and white chrysanthemums were planted beneath the cathedral's soaring buttresses in honor of the Pontiff, whose traditional colors are white and gold. The holy-water sprinkler that the Pope was to wield at the cathedral's entrance was carefully replated in gold. And, in the Cardinal's residence, the hand-carved papal throne that had stood unused since 1850 was made ready for use.

At midday, after making his one-minute speech of welcome, Cardinal Spellman followed respectfully behind as the Pope walked along the cathedral terrace, waving with both hands at the crowds. But the Pontiff paused to link arms with him and moved on, waving now only with his right arm. The Cardinal, who at 76 was short of step, tried to keep up with his leader's sweeping strides.

Together, they passed through the narrow rear door of the Cardinal's four-story residence. Flowers sent by the faithful brightened the somber Victorian chambers. Security officials kept watch in the ground floor, and Cardinal Spellman's three maids, dressed in black uniforms with white lace aprons, stood in attendance.

A security official said the Pope took the residence's small, halting elevator up to the third-floor guest suite set aside for him. He and an aide entered the suite—which smelled of fresh paint—and closed the door behind them. In the sitting room a television set was ready for his use. The residence staff had cleaned and dusted the furniture in the small bedroom and the bathroom, which has a tub with shower. The papal valet, Franco Chezzi, had arrived earlier with the vestments the Pope was to wear for mass.

After changing into a fresh white cassock, the Pope went on for his audience with the President, passing through the residence's Gothic front portal, which was decorated with his cartouche (coat-of-arms) and cloth in the papal colors. Cardinal Spellman stayed behind and, at 1:52 P.M., stepped laboriously down the front steps and stood in the cold sunlight on Madison Avenue, awaiting his guest's return.

Shortly before two o'clock, the papal limousine rolled up.

Cardinal Spellman, his pectoral cross gleaming in the sunlight, stood by the Pope during the unveiling of a polychromed bronze plaque attached to the residence wall. It read: "His Holiness Pope Paul VI on the occasion of his historic visit to the United Nations Assembly to deliver Christ's Message of Peace was a revered guest in this home of the Archbishops of New York, 4 October 1965."

At the ceremony, a member of the police guard, Patrolman James McDevitt of Brooklyn, kissed the Cardinal's ring—and was thunderstruck when the Pope, smiling, gave him the golden tassel from the cloth that had veiled the plaque.

Then Pope and Cardinal reentered the residence for a simple lunch at the oval table in the ground-floor dining room.

The Pope ate a substantial lunch provided by the Waldorf-Astoria Hotel. Bart Moore of the hotel's catering department said the meal had been taken over to the residence from the hotel kitchen, where it had been cooked by Eugene Scanlon, the executive chef.

At lunch the Pope was joined by Cardinal Spellman and a papal aide, Monsignor Pasquale Macchi. They ate off the Waldorf's "gold service" plates, using sterling silver bearing the Waldorf's crest.

Mr. Moore said the Pope ate everything served him. The meal consisted of hot, triple-strength chicken consomme, scallopine of veal with peas and mushrooms, mixed green salad and mixed chopped tropical fruits for dessert, with American coffee. Mr. Moore said no wine was served. He also said the hotel mixed a special salad dressing to suit the Pope's taste. He said he did not know the ingredients.

Shortly before three o'clock, Cardinal Spellman again appeared outside his door. Other cardinals in the papal party gathered on the sidewalk, and Cardinal Spellman gave them small boxes containing a gift: gold cufflinks.

At 3:05 P.M. the Pope emerged, this time wearing a red cloak. He drove off for the United Nations, again with Cardinal Spellman at his side.

They returned a few minutes before seven o'clock. A security official at the residence said the Pope went up to his apartment and rested. The Waldorf had made preparations to serve a supper of beef consomme followed by poultry and sherbet. But the Pontiff simply drank tea in his apartment, the official said, while the crowd outside chanted: "We want the Pope" and maids drew the blinds behind the residence's lace curtains.

At 8:16 the Pope emerged from the residence for the last time while, behind him, a monsignor helped Cardinal Spellman down the steps. The Pope and the Cardinal took their places in the limousine's capacious rear compartment, which was equipped with a tan thermos container for water and three simple drinking glasses, and were off to Yankee Stadium.

A monsignor on the Cardinal's staff said the papal throne in the residence, which had been turned around to face into the throne room, would now be turned again to face the wall, as it had for 115 years before Cardinal Spellman was host to the Pope.

Ancient Rites and Blessings

By Will Lissner

Pope Paul VI's day in New York, from his welcome at St. Patrick's Cathedral to his departure ceremony in the chapel of the Vatican Pavilion at the World's Fair, was full of rites, rituals and ceremonies, many with forms that go back 1,900 years.

The Pope made visits to the Blessed Sacrament at the cathedral, at Holy Family Church and at the pavilion chapel, just like any Catholic, layman or cleric. As he moved about he blessed according to the ordinary form the people he encountered, like any priest. He celebrated a pontifical mass at Yankee Stadium that was a mass such as any other bishop could celebrate.

But he bestowed one sacramental that was his alone of all

the clergy in the world to bestow—the Apostolic Benediction. Many New Yorkers not of the Roman Catholic faith received the Apostolic Benediction during the day, at the cathedral, the church, the United Nations, the mass or the pavilion. Some asked, what does it mean, does it mean anything to non-Catholics?

Blessings by scriptural tradition are expressions of a wish that all good fortune may go with the person blessed. Among Roman Catholics they are considered to be reserved to the clergy as sacramentals, that is, rituals or sacred things that help to deepen faith.

The greatest of the blessings are those given by bishops, who are revered by Catholics as direct successors of the apostles, the original followers of Jesus of Nazareth. And the greatest of these is the solemn blessing, the Apostolic Benediction, given by the Bishop of Rome, the Pope himself.

The formula for the blessing is the benediction that closes the mass in every church, "May Almighty God bless you, the Father, and the Son, and the Holy Spirit."

Roman Catholics believe that when they sin they owe divine justice satisfaction that they may repay temporally, provided they are truly contrite, by offering their troubles, sorrows and sufferings in retribution while doing their best to repair the harm they have done others.

They also believe that with the Apostolic Benediction they can earn what is called a plenary indulgence—remission of temporal punishment. They earn it by making a good confession in which they are truly penitent for their sins and really resolve to undergo conversion, to change their ways. In addition they must go to communion, offering its fruits for the intention of the Pope, that is, for divine guidance for peace.

Catholics believe that others can receive the benefit of the Pope's solemn good wishes if they choose to do so. The extent to which the blessing is beneficial to them, Catholics believe, is determined by the desire of the non-Catholics and the state of their conscience and their soul.

As for nonbelievers, for example agnostics, the blessing can be taken as an expression of goodwill, and its courteous acceptance as a response in goodwill. It does not compromise the recipient.

In the ceremonies at the cathedral and the Holy Family Church, Pope Paul VI acted just like any other Catholic visiting a strange church. What Catholics make is not a visit to the edifice but a devotional practice, which they call a visit to the

71

Blessed Sacrament, a visit to the presence of Jesus Christ in the Blessed Sacrament.

When Catholics enter a church, they dip the tips of the fingers of the right hand in a holy-water fount and touch the forehead, the chest, the left shoulder and the right (or if they are of the Eastern rite, the right shoulder and the left) in the sign of the Cross.

The sign is an ancient sacramental used by early Christians. The Pope blessed himself at St. Patrick's Cathedral and again at Holy Family Church. Then, being the superior prelate, he took an aspergillum, a gold-and-silver device from which holy water can be sprinkled, and blessed his party.

Then the Pope went to a kneeling stool called a prie-dieu and knelt before the tabernacle where consecrated bread is reserved as the Blessed Sacrament and said a private prayer of thanksgiving. At St. Patrick's his prayer was for a safe journey. At Holy Family, it was believed, it was for the opportunity to speak before the United Nations.

At St. Patrick's the Pope sat at the altar in the throne of honor, where normally Cardinal Spellman sits when he presides at mass. At Holy Family the Pope sat in a special throne that undoubtedly henceforth will be reserved for him and will become a historic part of the church.

The mass celebrated at Yankee Stadium was what Catholics used to call a *missa recitata*—a recited mass—before conversion of the rituals to the vernacular. It is now called a vernacular mass. Technically, it is the mass called in the Roman Missal a "votive mass for peace"—that is, a mass for the special intention of seeking divine guidance for peace.

The mass was called a pontifical mass because the Pope celebrated it. Normally such masses are celebrated by bishops or by monsignors who "pontificate," or wear the miter of a bishop by special appointment of the Pope.

It had been announced that the Pope would celebrate the mass in Latin. But the Pope followed the English form approved by the United States bishops. Thus the entrance rite, the so-called Kyrie from the Greek formerly used, was rendered by the Pope in English, "Lord have mercy, Christ have mercy, Lord have mercy."

The blessing before the reading of the collect in Latin, a collection of spiritual readings, was given also in Latin, *"Dominus vobiscum"* (the Lord be with you), and the response recited by the people was in Latin. *"Et cum spiritu tuo."* (And with thy spirit.) The Latin was retained in the English mass at this point.

The sermon given by the Pope at Yankee Stadium was a homily, that is, a moral exhortation. The bishops of the United States have directed that their priests give a homily whenever possible at every mass, except on certain special occasions when the sermon is reserved for instruction in dogma or in scripture.

With the introduction of the vernacular mass, readings from sacred scripture are given in English and expositions of scripture from the letters of the Apostles are also given in English. Thus there is less need for scriptural instruction in the sermon.

In only one respect the mass differed from a votive mass for peace offered by any of the United States bishops or, on special occasions during the year, by United States monsignors. As children brought bread and wine, and a dove, a symbol of peace, as gifts to the altar, the offering prayer and the prayer of the faithful were given not only in English but also in the four other official languages of the United Nations, French, Spanish, Russian and Chinese.

Members of United Nations delegations and of the secretariat recited the prayers.

The Pope said the eucharistic prayer, including the exhortation, *"Sursum corda"* (Lift up your hearts) in Latin, and then the people, standing, said in English the Sanctus: "Holy, holy, holy, Lord God of Hosts, heaven and earth are filled with your glory, hosanna in the highest, blessed is he who comes in the name of the Lord."

The solemn words of consecration of the bread as the body of Christ were given by the Pope in English, the Pontiff saying slowly and deliberately, "For this is my body." Similarly he consecrated the wine as the blood of Christ.

Then the Pope said the Lord's Prayer in English, and followed with the blessing Dominus Vobiscum also in English as "The Lord be with you." (This blessing is given at the beginning, the middle and at the end of the mass.)

When communion was given, the children selected to receive it on behalf of the congregation knelt, the former custom. Under reform of the liturgy communicants are supposed to remain standing, bowing and leaving to make their communion prayers of thanksgiving in their seats.

Bishop Bryan McEntegart of Brooklyn gave the dismissal, "Go, the mass is ended." in ringing English and then the Pope

73

gave the final blessing in Latin, and recited the final prayers in English.

The Pope used for the mass the crozier with which he opened the current session of Ecumenical Council Vatican II. It is not a shepherd's crook, like the croziers of most bishops, but a shepherd's staff surmounted by a crucifix with a readily seen corpus, the figure of the body of Christ on the Cross.

At the Vatican Pavilion at the Fair the Pope, like any tourist, admired the setting of the *Pietà,* Michelangelo's statue of 1498 depicting Mary holding the body of her son, Jesus, after it had been taken down from the cross. The work is from the Pope's church, St. Peter's Basilica in Rome.

Afterward, he greeted crowds in the chapel and other gathering places of the pavilion with his familiar wave and gave them his solemn Apostolic Benediction, using the Latin form: *"Benedicat vos omnipotens Deus, Pater et Filius, et Spiritus Sanctus"* (May Almighty God bless you: the Father, the Son, and the Holy Spirit).

Problems of Protocol

By PETER GROSE

The protocol of it all required elegant rationalizations by people who take such things seriously. Consider the difficulties:

The Pope is a chief of state, but the Vatican City is not recognized by the United States, nor is it a member of the United Nations.

The Pope is also the head of a church, and there are dozens of religious leaders who could claim equivalent status.

He came to the international territory of the United Nations, which is accorded privileges of extraterritoriality. But obviously he had to pass through United States territory to get to the United Nations headquarters on New York's East River.

The President of the United States is not a man to pass up a chance to talk with as distinguished a visitor as the Pope. But how does one arrange a meeting in New York without setting a precedent that could prove embarrassing when other visitors come?

Protocol officers of the United Nations, the Department of State and the Archbishopric of New York had answers to all the problems by the day the Pope came.

"The visit fell into a very special category," one government protocol expert said.

The basis for the arrangements was the Pope's status as a chief of state. Proceeding from that, the necessary explanations were devised.

Pope Paul VI did not pay a state visit to the United States. Normally a ceremonial visit by a chief of state follows the procedure of a state visit; that of a head of government, such as a prime minister, is called an official visit. The Pope's day in New York was neither, so the question of Washington's nonrecognition was dodged. Some officials believed the Pope deliberately kept the visit short to avoid diplomatic complications.

Nor did the Pope pay an official visit to the United Nations. He came as the guest of the Secretary-General, U Thant. This avoided the issue of the Vatican as not being a member of the international organization and, United Nations officials hope, also avoided setting a precedent on which other religious leaders could stake claims to similar visits.

As a courtesy of common sense, the United States government granted certain chief-of-state privileges to the Pope, whether his state is recognized or not.

There was no immigration officer at Kennedy International Airport to demand a papal passport. No customs officials asked to open the Pontiff's suitcases.

This facility originated in a formal request from the Department of State Protocol Office to the Bureau of Customs asking that formalities be waived as a courtesy.

For the question of the meeting with President Johnson, diplomatically innocent arrangements were hastily made. The President found it convenient to accept a dinner invitation at the New York apartment of his good friend the Representative at the United Nations, Arthur J. Goldberg, the night before the Pope arrived.

The President would thus be on hand at his suite in the Waldorf-Astoria the next day if the Pope cared to drop in.

President Kennedy visited the Pope in Rome in 1963—it was then Pope John XIII—so it was quite appropriate for the Pope to return the call.

Here is how all this intricate reasoning showed up during the visit:

The first person to greet Pope Paul VI when his plane touched down on American territory was the Holy See's Permanent Observer to the United Nations, the Right Reverend

Alberto Giovannetti. The Pope greeted him with outstretched hand just inside the aircraft.

Monsignor Giovannetti then beckoned to U Thant to mount the steps; the Pope and the Secretary-General shook hands in the doorway of the plane.

Mr. Thant then escorted his guest down the steps and presented him to officials who had gone to the airport to pay their respects, whether demanded by formal protocol or not. There was Amintore Fanfani, President of the General Assembly; Secretary of State Dean Rusk, Governor Rockefeller and Mayor Wagner.

The call on President Johnson was the only occasion during the visit on which the Pope fell under the responsibility of State Department protocol.

The President dispatched the Chief of Protocol, Lloyd Hand, to pick up his distinguished visitor. Mr. Hand escorted the Pope from the residence of Cardinal Spellman, Archbishop of New York, to the Waldorf-Astoria.

They rode up in the elevator together, and at the doorway of the presidential suite, Mr. Hand muttered, "May I present His Holiness, Pope Paul VI?"

It was the Pope calling on the President, so, naturally, it was the Pope who was presented to the President. "It was all rather nicely handled," one relieved protocol officer said.

Sharing the Financial Burden

By Sydney H. Schanberg

It was not a day for keeping books or worrying about money.

Though millions of dollars were spent on the papal visit—making it perhaps the costliest one-day trip in history—church officials and others were reluctant to talk about the costs, as though it would be sacrilegious in the context of the occasion.

Indeed, in a spirit of charity and noncommercialism, many of the services and facilities were donated, such as the use of Yankee Stadium for the pontifical mass.

The largest single expense was the cost of security. The New York City Police Department assigned about 15,000 of its nearly 27,000 men to the visit and estimated that the overtime bill would run to about one million dollars.

But this, too, was in a sense a donation—a gift from the taxpayers of New York.

The same was generally true of the thousands of dollars spent on extra guards and policemen from other agencies—the Housing Authority, Transit Authority, Port of New York Authority, United Nations and State Department.

Another contribution, this from the Ford Motor Company, was a fleet of eight cars for Pope Paul VI's motorcades through the city—including the two specially adapted bubble-top limousines that the Pontiff himself used alternately throughout the day.

The special information bureau set up by the Archdiocese of New York to handle all queries about the visit was also the product of helping hands.

Alcoa Plaza Associates donated the use of a fourth-floor wing of an office-apartment skyscraper it is building at 866 United Nations Plaza. Two private public-relations firms provided the organizational personnel for the bureau (Papal Visit News Center), and volunteers manned the telephones, typewriters and mimeograph machines.

Despite this assistance, the archdiocese still faced a sizable financial burden. For example, while the use of Yankee Stadium —for which the minimum one-day rental fee is $10,000—was free, the extras were not.

A two-and-a-half-story altar had to be erected for the mass, thousands of camp chairs had to be rented for extra seating on the stadium grass, a $25,000 red plush carpet also had to be rented to be placed around the altar and elsewhere in the stadium, 90,000 tickets had to be printed on a rush, overtime basis, and hundreds of ushers, ticket takers and guards had to be hired.

In almost every area of city life, the one-day visit had financial repercussions, but in most cases the effects were light.

Traffic congestion delayed truck deliveries to many stores, yet the Commerce and Industry Association estimated that this caused no significant harm to business.

The Transit Authority put on extra subway cars to and from Yankee Stadium and the Pontiff's other stopping points, but transit officials predicted that the extra riders would probably offset the cost.

The same prediction was made by the city's commuter railroads—the New Haven, the New York Central and the Long Island—all of which either added cars or made extra stops to handle the additional throngs of suburbanites seeking a glimpse of the Pope.

The air trip for the Pope and his party was paid for by the Vatican. On the trip from Rome to New York, made in an Alitalia jet, eighteen persons were in the party, including the Pope. On the trip back, by Trans World Airlines, there were twenty-one.

The cost for each was the regular first-class fare—$890.60 round trip and $468.70 for those who went only one-way.

The members of the press, who rode in the rear of the plane, paid the normal economy fare—$544.40 round trip and $286.50 one way.

For Alitalia, the cost of outfitting the plane with special papal appointments was negligible, since it was the same plane that carried the Pope on his visits to the Holy Land and India and was already specially adapted.

TWA, on the other hand, said it had to spend "several thousand dollars" to make similar changes on its plane.

Neither private companies nor church officials were eager to talk about specific costs. The members of the archdiocese staff of Cardinal Spellman, gave the impression that they considered money an improper subject on such a spiritual occasion.

Monsignor Patrick Ahern, the Cardinal's secretary, politely brushed off a reporter's question about expenses by saying: "We've been spending it without counting it. And people have been donating. We haven't added it all up. When we get the bill, we'll pay it."

A Spokesman for Man

By John Cogley

Pope Paul VI's appearance before the United Nations marks the beginning of a new era for the Roman Catholic Church and may signify a wider revolution in the relationship between religion and secular life.

The Pope, pleading for peace before the representatives of 117 nations, cast himself in the role of the ancient prophet— the man above merely national, racial or political loyalties.

It is a role utterly fitting for one whose chief title is the Vicar of Christ on earth. For the highest conception of the man called Jesus, even among those who do not accept the theological claims of Christianity, is that of one who stood for the noblest aspirations of the human spirit—aspirations that transcend everything that divides, and ultimately dishonors, humanity.

Pope Paul VI, with the great prestige of the papacy backing up his words, chose to speak of peace and brotherhood, emphasizing that which unites and passing over those things that still divide mankind in an age of sharp ideological and religious differences.

It was not that the Pontiff put himself forth as an absolute neutral in the ideological wars that have brought such misery on the men of our time. His own creed, known to all the world, was neither sacrificed nor left open for barter during his speech.

No one left the United Nations believing that the Pope of Rome had suddenly and unaccountably become an indifferentist in the battles being waged on the ideological level for the soul of man.

The present pope remains as adamantly opposed to atheistic and relativistic systems of thought as any of his predecessors.

What has happened is that the Pope has chosen to become a spokesman for man. It was the survival of mankind and the peace and well-being of man that he emphasized in his speech.

Like his forerunner, the beloved Pope John XXIII, Pope

Paul VI realizes that science and technology have annulled any purpose that warfare in the past might have served. In his encyclical "Pacem in Terris" (Peace on Earth) Pope John pleaded again and again for reason and common sense to be put ahead of ideological claims and did so, not in the name of Platonic abstractions, but in the name of the survival of the creatures of flesh and blood who inhabit the earth.

Pope Paul VI has taken up where Pope John XXIII left off.

The change from even the recent past is that the Pope no longer seems to look upon his church as a party in the world's quarrels or as a political partisan of any kind, but as a spiritual force upholding human dignity and the goodness of life.

Not too many years ago the Roman Catholic Church was looked upon by the Western powers as a quasi-political ally. There has been a tremendous change. Ecumenical Council Vatican II, for example, has carefully refrained from condemning Communism by name.

The present mood of Catholicism is to suspect its own power. Many of the present leaders are trying to break with the church's political past and to recapture its original purity.

This is not easily achieved. Pope Paul VI, even as he spoke of his own lack of political power, must have realized that his words were still fraught with political significance. They will be read and analyzed as carefully as any ruler's.

For example, the simple reference to birth control in the Pontiff's speech—the suggestion that the United Nations should concern itself more with the distribution of the world's goods than the control of population—will be invested with tremendous political significance.

It will suggest to many observers that the Roman Catholic Church, despite recent hopes ignited by the Ecumenical Council, will continue to block efforts to control population by governmental action. Many in the Pope's vast audience, however, are convinced that in an age of medical advance, control of overpopulation, without widespread contraception, is as hopeless as trying to hold off war while armaments grow more widespread and more fierce.

In the main, the Pope's speech will make life easier for those harassed statesmen who are trying to avoid violence and war. By removing the church and, by extension, the force of religious zeal from the political energies of the cold war, the Pontiff may have cooled fires that frequently threaten to get out of hand.

By throwing his vast prestige and spiritual authority behind the United Nations, he strengthened the one means for peaceful settlement of burning political issues open to contemporary man.

Like his predecessor, Pope Paul VI seemed to be saying that before man can believe in God, he must first believe in himself. In this sense, his speech was a thundering credo—worthy of the great churchmen.

An Exalted Voice

By James Reston

For the first time since the death of Winston Churchill, the nation's capital has been startled out of its normal routine by the power of an exalted voice.

"The hour has struck for a halt," said Pope Paul VI, "a moment of recollection, of reflection, almost of prayer; a moment to think anew of our common origin, our history, our common destiny."

Washington seldom thinks steadfastly about the human family as a whole. It deals in personalities, in political parties, in nations, or at most in alliances and enemies, but for a few moments the Pope gave it a vision of the common human pilgrimage.

It was not that he said anything new—on the United Nations, birth control, hunger or war—but simply that he said a lot of old fundamental things that have been overwhelmed for so long that they sounded new again.

Lately, there has been so much talk of war in Vietnam, war in India and Pakistan, rebellion in Indonesia, marines in the Dominican Republic, and squabbling in the western alliance, that the pontiff's simple human cry of "no more war, war never again!" is almost startling.

It seems a long time ago that men were talking passionately about the scrambling disorder of the world and calling for disarmament and a great creative effort to establish a world authority and get some unity of purpose and a common control of human affairs. Yet here was this spare and majestic man appealing with his calm voice and graceful hands for just these things.

John Foster Dulles, of all people, was the last influential man around here to talk of a "universal" United Nations, including Communist China, but here was the Pope suggesting, with the utmost delicacy, that the members of the United Nations "study the right method of uniting to your pact of brotherhood, in honor and loyalty, those who do not yet share it."

Pope Paul VI called his address to the United Nations "a solemn ratification of this lofty institution." The U.N., he added, must never fail. "Let unanimous trust in this institution grow, let its authority increase. . . ."

"Is there anyone," he asked, "who does not see the necessity of coming thus progressively to the establishment of a world authority, able to act efficaciously on the juridical and political levels?"

The political significance of this in the United States is plain enough. There are indeed a great many people in this country, including many influential politicians of the Roman Catholic faith, who regard the U.N. as a communist trap, who do not want to see its authority or its membership increased, and who specifically do not favor turning it into a powerful "world authority."

The Pope, however, all but created an alliance between the spiritual authority of the Roman Catholic Church, and the temporal authority of the United Nations—all but on the subject of birth control.

Here the spiritual and temporal worlds of these two institutions seemed to part. The U.N. is profoundly concerned about the rapid growth of the human race. Over half of the people of the world are now suffering from malnutrition, and the U.N. demographers estimate that world population will double by the end of this century to 6 billion.

In eighty five countries of Africa, Asia and Latin America, the U.N. estimates that only one half of the 250 million primary age children are enrolled in schools, so that every year about 20 million are added to the illiterate adult population, which already includes 40 per cent of the world's population.

Accordingly, the U.N. is encouraging population control by artificial means, and the Johnson Administration is cooperating when requested in these and other similar programs.

The Pope took a somewhat different view. "The life of man is sacred," he said. "No one may dare offend it. Respect for life, even with regard to the great problem of birth, must find here in your assembly its highest affirmation and its most reasoned defense.

"You must strive to multiply bread so that it suffices for the tables of mankind, and not rather favor an artificial control of birth, which would be irrational, in order to diminish the number of guests at the banquet of life."

Banquet? The word sent a gasp around Washington. For there is a fundamental issue here. There is no quarrel with the Pope's statement that "It does not suffice to feed the hungry; it is necessary also to assure to each man a life conformed to his dignity," and this is precisely the point of conflict.

For the U.N. is operating on the assumption that human life should be controlled until by artificial means there is some reasonable expectation of providing both food and dignity to each person, whereas the Pope seemed to be emphasizing once more that artificial birth control was "irrational."

Officials in the capital were surprised that the Pope took this position while the Roman Catholic Church was in the process of drafting a definitive statement of policy on this subject, but they noted that much would depend on whether the church regarded birth control pills as "artificial" or as "natural" devices.

There was also some surprise here that Pope Paul VI did not say more about the obligation of the rich industrial nations of the northern hemispheres to provide more help to the poor agricultural nations of the southern hemispheres.

Again, United Nations officials are troubled by what they regard as a growing class struggle between the rich nations and the poor nations, and they would have been pleased if their distinguished visitor had given more emphasis to the urgent need to deal, not only with wars, but with the economic and social causes of wars.

The Pope's mission as a whole, however, was regarded in Washington and in New York as a great success. In the twenty years since the formation of the world organization, there have been few such memorable days.

Vision and Reality of the U.N.

BY ARTHUR KROCK

Pope Paul VI spoke for all the enlightened members of the human race when he pleaded for the fulfillment of his vision of a United Nations "able to act efficaciously on the juridical and political levels" for the attainment and preservation of world peace.

This is the ideal on which the U.N. was conceived.

His call for a search for "the right method of uniting to your pact of brotherhood . . . those who do not yet share in it" repeated another ideal and aspiration of the U.N.'s conception. But, though the spiritual leader of the largest religious denomination of the West cannot involve himself in the inevitably controversial details of any program which might be advanced for the fulfillment of his vision, the Pope's evocation of it before the members of the international organization brings these enormous difficulties vividly to mind.

How, for example, can the United Nations "act efficaciously on the juridical and political levels" until the equal voting weight of all members of the assembly is recast to reflect some practical proportion of the will and power of the governments and peoples represented in the assembly? So long as the assembly vote of the weakest, most blindly nationalistic or autocratic government carries the same weight in the decision as those of the strongest who have demonstrated their commitment to comity among the nations, the effectiveness of the U.N. on these levels cannot be achieved.

How can it be achieved in the presence of a Security Council where the veto of any permanent member can nullify the agreement of all the others on the imposition of diplomatic and economic sanctions (as well as military) against even the most flagrant violation of the Charter by a member nation? Conversely, if it were possible to excise the veto power from the Charter, which it is not, how could the U.N. be held together as a world organization, effective or otherwise, on any "level?"

Furthermore, how can the organization attain effectiveness in even the limited areas, as specified by the Pope, without including the government of Communist China, which rigidly controls a large percentage of the world's population?

Only by a military concert of the great powers, by which the Peiping regime or a bloody internal revolution could be overthrown. Or by a revision of Peiping to a policy of peaceful cooperation and nonaggression.

The vision of Pope Paul VI, who ex-officio is the expounder of human progress by peaceful means alone, could not conceivably include the first two solutions. It may be that the Pope's concept of a "right method" of adhering Communist China to the U. N. "brotherhood" does not exclude the theory many hold—that admission would imbue Peiping with a resolve to try out the philosophy of peace. But until this theory is supported by some substantial evidence, it is a vision, too.

These and other and more immediate difficulties the U.N. must surmount before it can make any realistic progress toward attainment of the moderate role invoked for it by Paul VI.

For instance, there is the armed combat over Kashmir between India and Pakistan.

The dispute is ideally one which should be soluble on "juridical and political levels." But practically, it has reached an impasse where only external international force—military as well as economic—could impose a fair and peaceful settlement on both parties. And, because of the built-in limitation of the U.N., and the menacing outsider in Peiping, it cannot effect that any more than it can effect it on the nonmilitary levels specified by the Pope.

The United States is as much to blame as the great Communist world mischief makers for another source of weakness in the U.N., a guilt compounded by the constant overselling of the organization by the last four administrations. It is the United States' official attitude, resting on the imaginary base of "world opinion," that revolutions are always constructive and desirable if they are not clearly designed to increase the territorial control of Russian or Chinese Communism. That has enabled Moscow and Peiping to confuse and paralyze the peace-keeping and peace-restoring machinery of the U. N., and gain an advantage in the propaganda of the cold war, by hailing and supporting revolutions in their interest as "wars of liberation."

The Dilemma of Church Art

By John Canaday

The two churches visited by Pope Paul VI during his day in New York could not have been better chosen if the idea had been to demonstrate the dilemma of church art today. St. Patrick's Cathedral, begun in 1858, is proof that the forms of the Age of Faith cannot be exhumed in the modern era without seeming to be what, indeed, they are—embalmed. And the newly dedicated Holy Family Church at 323 East 47th Street is proof that contemporary industrial forms cannot be translated successfully to serve the expression of faith.

In the eighty-six years since St. Patrick's was formerly opened, it has become a loved monument, and it has many virtues. Form by form—from pier to pier, from window to window, from vault to vault—it is a respectful and scholarly re-creation of a Gothic cathedral, but it is not a Gothic cathedral for all that. Its extreme regularity, achieved by modern building methods, gives it the mechanical dryness of any other good copy; it has none of the living mystery of a true Gothic cathedral except as we supply it by association. As an architectural expression of a living religion, St. Patrick's is as meaningless as a mass celebrated by robots: the building is consummately a proof that all the forms of spiritual expression may be copied, but that the spirit itself may be lacking hopelessly and forever.

If the church operated today on the architectural premise involved in St. Patrick's, theology would be frozen into the philosophies of the thirteenth century, which, while they were alive and growing, inspired the alive and growing architecture of the cathedrals. If it is born alive, as the medieval cathedrals were, a building never dies, but nothing can bring a stillborn building to life. And St. Patrick's, for all its beauty and for all the affection in which we hold it, was architecturally still-born.

Dedicated by Cardinal Spellman last March, the Holy Family Church is an effort to bring church architecture and decoration to life by means of an impossible philosophical broad jump spanning seven centuries—to express the modernity of the church in terms of modern style. But in such efforts the architects and designers are necessarily licked from the start. The building, designed by George J. Sale of New York, presents a flat façade as sleek as any office skyscraper's, pierced by an entrance of such ostentatious simplicity that without foreknowledge of your whereabouts you would think that you had gained admission not to a house of God but to the inner sanctum of some multimillion-dollar industrialist. Beyond the lobby, the church itself has much the same air in spite of the religious subjects of its sculpture and stained glass.

The window pictures and the ceramic and metal bas-reliefs on the walls are determinedly modern in a simplified, angular style that is already dated. Esthetically they have the discreetly chic flavor of seventy-five cent Christmas cards where something thought of as good taste is confused with mere asepsis. And on the end wall a large bronze figure of Christ, or a large bronze manikin purporting to be a figure of Christ, is lamentably a demonstration of the divorce between the church and the arts today. Although it is about as good as these semi-modern, semitraditional sculptures get, the figure is spiritually so hollow that you feel it would give a tinny ring if tapped with a knuckle, and no sense of sacrilege would be involved in thus tapping it as an experiment.

The saddest thing is that these architects and designers serving an age of industry have obviously done their level best to force their talents into an appropriately religious expression, but their failure is apparent when the Holy Family Church is contrasted with the simplest structure built by journeymen architects and decorated by provincial artisans of the Age of Faith. These true churches are filled with a living hush. The silence is vibrant. But you can be alone in the Holy Family Church, with all street noises shut out, and you are merely surrounded by dead stillness.

Contemporary church design of this kind is based on an insurmountable disharmony. The forms that have grown so naturally in our century to serve industry can serve religion only as last-ditch expedients. They speak of machines, of knowhow, of hardheadedness and practicality as a way of life, of moneymaking as a philosophical goal. To try to use them as religious forms is as irrational as to try to house a General Motors assembly line in the Cathedral of Chartres. And no irreverence is possible in recognizing the Holy Family Church as a failure. The irreverence would be in imagining that these sterilized, hackneyed adaptations of a living architecture are visual embodiments of the progressive spirit of the church today, or that St. Patrick's symbolizes the church as an institution fettered to the past.

The flat fact is that, for reasons a theologian, a sociologist and an esthetician might be able to unravel by joint efforts, the modern church and the modern architect-artist are simply unable to communicate with—and through—one another.

TV Spectacular

By Jack Gould

Millions of viewers in more than twenty-two countries on two continents saw the striking live television coverage of the visit of Pope Paul VI to New York.

It was a day and evening of unforgettable visual contrasts

on the home screen as the television industry mobilized the greatest amount of technical equipment and manpower ever assigned to the electronic reporting of an event. The New York Telephone Company said the demand for communications of facilities for the event had exceeded the combined requirements for the funeral of President Kennedy and the five Gemini space shots.

Virtually every moment of the Pope's public appearances was caught in remarkable pictorial detail as more than eighty-five cameras were used to follow his fourteen-hour stay in the city.

Between 100 million and 200 million persons in the United States, Canada and Mexico were expected to see some portion of the TV coverage while at least 200 million persons in Britain and Western Europe watched pictures relayed by the Early Bird satellite.

In addition, thousands of radio stations throughout the world carried the Pope's address to the United Nations.

The legendary ability of television to personalize a moment of history found repeated expression in a series of intimate vignettes about the Pontiff.

There was an unforgettable closeup of his face as he murmured a prayer of thanksgiving for his safe arrival. The solitary figure in white, seen against the dark interior of St. Patrick's Cathedral, might have been a painting in all its moving starkness. The longer views of the main aisle of St. Patrick's, as the Pope walked toward the sanctuary to the applause of those in attendance, were gems of pictorial composition.

Later, at the Waldorf-Astoria, there was an absorbing scene of the Pope and President Johnson in conversation. For the viewer it represented a fascinating study of differing personalities, the President talking animatedly and the Pope listening intently. No sound pickup of the exchange was allowed, so the two worlds could only be watched in pantomime, a novel way to witness history in the making.

So meticulous was television's planning that the viewer was able to see the Pope in a variety of other informal moments, such as trying to open the car door upon his arrival at Cardinal Spellman's residence or smiling gently upon seeing a friend.

One of the day's more poignant television scenes was Pope Paul VI's greeting of Mrs. John F. Kennedy at the reception at the United Nations after he had delivered his appeal for peace. They spoke in French.

Compared with the excellent photography of the Pope's

arrival in mid-Manhattan the coverage of the motorcade journey from Kennedy International Airport to St. Patrick's was disappointing. The chill wind, which forced the Pope to transfer to an enclosed car, thwarted television's hopes of gaining many closeups along the way.

From early morning until after the Pope's address at the United Nations, all regular television schedules were canceled by the American Broadcasting Company, Columbia Broadcasting System and National Broadcasting Company. There were no commercials during that coverage of the Pope.

All the networks shared the same pooled pictures, which were presented in what is known as "international" or "natural" sound. This meant that the commentaries were kept separate from the pictures so that the announcers for different countries could add their own reports in their own languages. The television systems of major European countries and Mexico had commentators sending back reports to their audiences.

The Early Bird satellite enabled American audiences to witness the Pope's departure from Rome. Films were also made as he visited the crowded press section of the Italian jetliner that brought his party to New York.

To supplement the reports of their regular staff members the networks arranged for the services of Roman Catholic priests to round out their accounts and appraise the Pope's trip.

Late in the afternoon C.B.S. made a journalistic decision that assumed viewers in New York had greater interest in the Pope's visit than viewers elsewhere. It resumed live coverage at 7:30 P.M. in New York while offering regular entertainment programs to its affiliated stations in other sections of the country.

A.B.C. carried *12 O'Clock High* both in New York and elsewhere at 7:30. N.B.C. carried coverage of the Pope on all outlets at 7:30. During regular newscasts and entertainment shows the networks carried commercials.

The three networks rejoined the TV pool for the mass at 8:30. The telecast of the mass, in color, was one of the viewing highlights of the day. The sanctuary erected in the center of the stadium was covered with soft red carpeting. The carpeting was also used for a mammoth aisle extending from the area of home plate out to the sanctuary. The corners of the sanctuary were bordered with hundreds of yellow chrysanthemums. A golden canopy covered the altar.

Because of widely varying lighting conditions in the stadium the color tended to be uneven but the over-all scene was one of rare pageantry. The closeups of nuns, cardinals, seminarians and members of the lay audience provided a succession of arresting pictures.

The mass was covered live by all New York City television stations except WOR-TV, which presented *The Million Dollar Movie* with its usual commercial spot announcements.

The Birth-Control Question

The impression in Rome of Pope Paul VI's references to birth control in his United Nations speech was that they were an indication of the trend of his thinking, but not a final ruling.

In effect, the Pontiff merely restated the traditional teaching of the Roman Catholic Church on birth control—that any artificial means of contraception is illicit. To some, the Pope seemed to close the way to any revision of the church's teaching. But others still awaited his formal declaration on the issue, a declaration he is expected to make later in the year.

Many expressed surprise that the Pontiff should have chosen the United Nations—a political forum in which there are many who do not recognize him as universal teacher—to make a declaration on such a controversial issue which is only peripheral to his main subject of peace.

However, it was noted that population control is on the General Assembly agenda for this session. The item, entitled "Population Growth and Economic Development: Report of the Economic and Social Council," is to be taken up first by the Economic Committee.

What the Pope said at the United Nations was this:

> . . . *the life of man is sacred; no one may dare offend it. Respect for life, even with regard to the great problem of the birth rate, must find here in your assembly its highest affirmation and its most reasoned defense. You must strive to multiply bread so that it suffices for the tables of mankind, and not rather favor an artificial control of birth, which would be irrational, in order to diminish the number of guests at the banquet of life."*

The key word in the passage, and in fact the key word in the current debate in the church over birth control, is "artificial." For, in the minds of many liberals, it has not been finally determined whether the anovulent birth-control pill that is at the center of the debate is an artificial contraceptive. It has been argued that the pill merely reinforces the natural reproductive cycle rather than artificially interfering with it.

The Pope's eagerly awaited formal declaration on the issue is expected to deal with the problem. Until the solemn document is promulgated, it is argued, any attempt to interpret other statements can only be speculation.

Before his elevation to the papacy, the Pontiff was associated with the traditionalist view of birth control. In June, 1964, however, he surprised many by appointing a papal commission of clergy and laymen and women to advise him on the problem.

In October and November, 1964, there was debate at the Second Vatican Council about contraception. A number of liberal prelates took the stand and pleaded for relief for the many Catholic families that had been burdened by the church's negative stand on population control. It seemed that the Council might take upon itself the task of revising or reaffirming the teaching of the church.

Early in 1965, however, it became apparent that the Pope would himself make a declaration on the subject outside the structure of the council. Presumably, such a declaration would take the form of a *motu proprio,* a comment on doctrinal matters issued on a pope's own initiative. Such a declaration is binding on all Catholics.

Beside his comments at the United Nations, Pope Paul has made three other observations on the vexing problem of birth control since he assumed the papacy on June 30, 1963.

In the summer of 1964, at the time he appointed his papal commission, he told Catholics to observe the ban on artificial contraception, reaffirmed by Pope Pius XII, until the commission could make recommendations to him. Liberals regarded this as a ray of light, because the Pontiff at least acknowledged the possibility of a change in the church's traditional position.

In the spring of 1965, addressing members of the commission during their meeting in Rome, Pope Paul VI urged them to make haste in reaching an agreement on its recommendations. Millions of the faithful, he indicated, found the issue of birth control one that deeply affected their personal lives and on which they sought new guidance.

His United Nations statement followed by one day an unusual interview with an Italian journalist in which the Pontiff stated that he found the issue most difficult to decide. Therefore, most observers concluded, his remarks in the General Assembly during his visit were merely a restatement of current church doctrine rather than an announcement of a new decision based on the recommendations he has had made by the commission of experts.

A Cautious Innovator

By Robert C. Doty

"His name is a program," said an observer when Giovanni Battista Montini chose to be known as "Paul" on his election to the papacy two years ago. His selection of the name of the great Apostle to the Gentiles was the expression of his desire to further Christian unity and to carry the word of Jesus to elements of modern society that appeared to have lost touch with them.

The slender, ascetic spiritual leader of half a billion Roman Catholics has also been actively dedicated to the material needs of mankind. Eight years before his elevation to the papacy, he expressed his social philosophy in these words: "No man must lack bread, a roof over his head, clothing and work. All who guide politics and economics must, in honor, make every effort to see that this aim is realized."

The sixty-eight-year-old Pontiff has keyed his own reign to the character of his three immediate predecessors, all of whom he has pledged to emulate—"Pius XI for his strong will, Pius XII for his knowledge and wisdom, John XXIII for his limitless goodness."

It is too early in his reign, according to observers at the Vatican, to draw any firm conclusions on whether the Pope has achieved this difficult mixture. Romans say it takes at least three years to make a pope. For a complicated, introspective, cautious intellectual like Pope Paul VI, it might take considerably longer for his image to crystallize.

In manner, personality and intellect he resembles most closely, thus far, his long-time patron, Eugenio Pacelli, Pope Pius XII. Like Pope Pius XII, he is austere and finds it difficult to establish warm, spontaneous human contacts.

There is some of the earlier pope, too, in Pope Paul VI's frequent, semidefensive assertions of papal supremacy in confrontation with the present thrust of the church's bishops in the Ecumenical Council toward "collegial" rule of the church.

Many observers, lay and clerical, are convinced that Pope

Paul VI does, indeed, share the aspirations of Pope John XXIII for renewal of the church. They believe that after the current council, Pope Paul VI will truly begin his own reign and achieve Pope John XXIII's ends with his own wide knowledge of the church and the world and his administrative and diplomatic skill.

There are others, however, who argue that the present pontiff sometimes acts as though he believes that Pope John XXIII's plans to "revitalize" the church have gone too far and that the time has come now to consolidate rather than to extend the program of change.

In his twenty-seven months on the throne of Peter, the Pope has disappointed those who saw in him one who would give unqualified endorsement to the progressive initiatives of his predecessor. Critics in the progressive majority of the Ecumenical Council charge that he has been too easily swayed by pressure of the conservative Curia and that his desire to preserve church "unity" by seeking to create a consensus among mutually hostile forces has produced uncertainty and confusion where strong leadership was needed.

His critics contend that his tendency is to "consult, consult, consult" and "reflect, reflect, reflect." The Pope is puzzled by these criticisms. In an interview with a French priest he asked: "Don't I have a right to reflect?"

Even his critics note, however, that Pope Paul VI has made spectacular departures from tradition. His trip to New York marked the first visit of a Pope to the New World, a trip that was preceded by another historic voyage in January, 1964, when his visit to the Holy Land marked the first such pilgrimage by a Roman pontiff since Christianity was born there nearly two thousand years ago. The trip to the Holy Land was the first in which a ruler of the Roman Catholic Church ever traveled by plane.

Moreover, it has been in his reign that revolutionary measures to modernize church liturgy have been approved against the vigorous opposition of the church's conservative wing.

Pope Paul VI—Bishop of Rome and Vicar of Jesus Christ, Successor of St. Peter, Prince of the Apostles, Supreme Pontiff of the Universal Church, Patriarch of the West, Primate of Italy, Archbishop and Metropolitan of the Roman Province, Sovereign of Vatican City—was born into a landholding upper-middle-class family at Concesio, near Brescia in northern Italy, on September 26, 1897.

The second of three sons of a lawyer who was a crusading

Catholic editor, the future pope was dogged by physical frailty through much of his boyhood and early youth. He received most of his early education privately at home, qualifying for a degree from the Brescia Lyceo—equivalent to a junior college—in 1916. Little is known of his boyhood experiences, except for recollections by acquaintances that a favorite activity was tree climbing.

He was rejected for military service in World War I because of his health. He began his study for the priesthood during this period and was ordained in Brescia in May, 1920. After his ordination he asked his bishop for permission to study further in Rome.

"You look exhausted," the Bishop told the fragile-looking priest. "Go to Rome, study a bit, yes, but eat some pasta and get some sleep and rest. Then come back here, and we'll see what you can do."

He heeded at least the study part of the Bishop's advice. After serving briefly as a parish priest, Father Montini entered Rome's Gregorian University for postgraduate studies. He caught the eye of a curial official, now Guiseppe Cardinal Pizzardo, who sent him to the Vatican's training school for diplomats.

After his graduation in 1923 he was sent to Warsaw as a junior in the papal nunciature there, but the severities of a Polish winter were too much for his fragile health and he returned to Rome the same year. For the next thirty-one years, until his nomination as Archbishop of Milan in 1954, he worked through the various levels of the Vatican secretariat, acquiring a reputation as diligent, discreet, efficient.

For part of this period, the future pope served as spiritual adviser to the Italian Federation of Catholic University Students. He resisted Fascist encroachments on the youth movement by advising noncooperation and nonviolence. But sometimes his nonviolence took strange shape; he is known to have waded into street fights when members of the youth movement were attacked by Fascist gangs. One federation veteran has offered his own recollection of the times: "Nobody hit him, because he was so skinny it looked as if you could blow him over, but the Fascists didn't know that what looked like a feather was a steel rod."

After Mussolini outlawed the student movement the future pope continued to meet with the students and conducted mass for them in the catacombs of Rome, the subterranean refuges of the early Christians.

His long association with Cardinal Pacelli—who became Pope Pius XII—began in 1930 when the Cardinal was Secretary of State for the Vatican. Under Cardinal Pacelli's patronage, the future Pope Paul VI had been advanced by 1937 to the rank of Substitute for Ordinary Affairs, one of the two principal posts under the Secretary of State. Two years later, his influence on Vatican affairs began to move out of the realm of anonymity and into public view, when Cardinal Pacelli was chosen Pope.

Operating from a three-room, third-floor office in the Vatican, the future pope became the principal executor of policy laid down by the Pontiff. In the final years of World War II, for example, he was deeply involved in the Vatican's numerous diplomatic exchanges with the combatants of both sides.

After the war he was in the forefront of the church's move for strong resistance to Italian Communism and its support for the Christian Democratic party.

Until December 12, 1954, most of Father Montini's life was devoted to service of the church at its administrative heart. Then he was consecrated Archbishop of Milan with great ceremony in St. Peter's Cathedral. A month later the new archbishop made a moving gesture of humility as he reached the border of his new see. Stepping from his car, he knelt and kissed the frozen ground.

Once in industrial Milan the Archbishop showed an unexpected flair for the poetic image. He declared: "I pray that the noise of machines becomes music and the smoke of chimneys incense."

His stay was notable for his efforts to win northern Italy's Marxists and Communists over to his own "doctrine of Christian love." He supported the worker-priest movement in France even after the conversion of several priests to Marxism brought the experiment official disfavor.

On December 15, 1958, four years after his consecration as Archbishop, he was proclaimed Cardinal, the first created by Pope John XXIII. Then, after Pope John XXIII's death, Cardinal Montini was elected Pope on June 21, 1963. Nine days later he was crowned in traditional ceremonies at the Vatican.

There is uncertainty over precisely where Pope Paul VI belongs in the numerical succession in his title as Successor of St. Peter. He has been variously described as the 261st, the 262d and the 263d Pontiff. The *National Catholic Almanac* notes that confusion exists in the numerical listing because of the questioned legitimacy of some claims to the pontificate in the church's long and sometimes schismatic history.

A voracious reader, Pope Paul sent a five-word message quickly to Milan following his elevation to the papacy: "Please send me my books." They arrived in ninety packing cases. He is said to quote as easily from a work by Thomas Mann or Oswald Spengler as from St. Thomas Aquinas. He enjoys fine music (notably Mozart, Beethoven, Brahms and Chopin) and listens often to high-fidelity recordings.

Little is known of his private life in the lonely splendor of the Vatican. He works on a grueling schedule, involving audiences, consultations and the writing and delivery of eight to ten speeches a week. He manages to go for long periods with only four hours of sleep a night, although he tries to get a nap during the day. He takes his breakfast in the continental fashion—rolls, butter, jam and coffee. He does not smoke, but enjoys Piedmontese wines with his meals.

Those who have long known him say that his dark eyes seem to have sunk deeper, his pale face to have taken on new lines and his slight figure to have become a bit more stooped since he assumed the keys of Peter.

Actions Etch an Image

By George Barrett

The sign of the Cross he traced in air, the vigorous stride that swirled the folds of his long cassock and the direct—almost piercing—look from his deep-set eyes—these are the images that Pope Paul VI engraved in memories during his visit to New York.

The Pontiff, a man of fragile physique, set a pace in his visit that scores of younger members in his retinue were hard pressed to maintain. His step throughout the taxing day was always quick, and his glances darted sharply.

For the United Nations, where the cocktail-party technique of the inattentive eye has been developed into a special trade skill, the Pope's insistence on looking directly and exclusively at his partner in conversation frequently proved disconcerting. Those who waited to engage the Pope could not catch his attention in advance; they were forced to wait while the Pontiff satisfied himself with each encounter.

It was rare when language was a problem. The Pope used three languages—English, French and Italian—as he passed down the waiting-lines and moved from one group to the next.

His hands never ceased their movement—clasping other hands in firm greeting, extending jointly in sweeping benedictions, lingering on the heads of youngsters lined up to meet him.

There was almost a language in the expressive movements. The wave of his right hand as he emerged from his plane at Kennedy Airport was an eager salute. Again and again he carved a cross with his right hand, and when the crowds applauded he extended both palms upward, pumping them repeatedly.

For Roman Catholics he placed his right hand palm down so they could kiss the papal ring; to those of other faiths he reached easily and naturally for a handshake.

The direct approach never died. He was delighted to stop for a moment to exchange personal greetings.

Many who watched the face of the Pontiff commented that his smile was what they would most vividly remember. Some called it gentle, others said it was a smile of joy, but many decided that the best description was "serene."

Pope Paul VI's Wide Range of Interests: His Own Words

Following are quotations from speeches and writings of the Pope, reflecting his views on a variety of topics:

In an audience with President Kennedy at Vatican City on July 2, 1963, the Pope recalled his 1960 trip to the United States as Archbishop of Milan:

We have visited your beautiful land, and as we traveled from one great city to another, we were able to experience personally the many admirable qualities which have made yours a leading member of the family of nations. . . . The untiring striving to obtain world peace is to be commended highly, and we are confident that these labors will find a ready response in all men of goodwill.

* * *

Appealing for peace, the Pope said in his first encyclical, issued August 10, 1964:

> *We shall be ready to intervene, where an opportunity presents itself, in order to assist the contending parties to find honorable and fraternal solutions for their disputes.*

* * *

Explaining his increasing the College of Cardinals from 76 to 103, at a Vatican ceremony on January 27, 1965:

> *The proportions of the church are no longer those of the Sixteenth century, but they have greatly grown and have expanded, thanks be to God, over the face of the earth.*

* * *

Commenting at the Vatican on the adoption of liturgical reforms, March 17, 1965:

> *Before it was enough to attend [mass]. Today it is necessary to participate. Before someone could doze and perhaps chat. Today, no. One must listen and pray.*

* * *

Outlining the goals of his papacy in his first address as Pope over the Vatican radio, June 22, 1963:

> *The preeminent part of our pontificate will be occupied by the continuation of the Ecumenical Council Vatican II, on which the eyes of all men of goodwill are focused.*

* * *

One of his first messages as Pope, sent to his former archdiocese in Milan, June 21, 1963:

> *Please send me my books.*

* * *

Discussing the church in his coronation homily, July 1, 1963:

> *We will try to preserve and increase the pastoral virtue of the church, which keeps her free and poor as mother and teacher, most loving of her faithful children, repsectful, comprehending and patient, and warmly calling to those who are not her children.*

* * *

Commenting on the meaning of the Ecumenical Council, at a 1964 audience with Père Antoine Wenger, editor of *La Croix*, Paris Catholic daily newspaper:

> *The eyes of faith must be kept focused not on mere appearances, but on the real meaning of the Council, which is a mystery. The plan of the Holy Spirit is not immedi-*

ately evident in the many episodes that make up the day-to-day business of the Council. But we know that it is an hour of grace, a great moment in the history of the church. Like the striking of the hour, it is preceded and followed by silence.

* * *

Instructing a special commission to study the issue of birth control, meeting at the Vatican, March 27, 1965:

The problem [birth control] posed can be summarized thus: In what form and according to what norms should married couples accomplish, in the exercise of their mutual love, that service to life to which their vocation calls them?

* * *

Appealing for an end to poverty in an address at the Thirty-eighth International Eucharistic Congress in Bombay, December 5, 1964:

Would that every nation, thinking thoughts of peace and not of affliction and war, would contribute even a part of its expenditure for arms to a great world fund for the relief of many problems of nutrition, clothing, shelter and medical care. . . .

* * *

An earlier appeal to end poverty, in a 1955 address to Christian workers while Archbishop of Milan:

No man must lack bread, a roof over his head, clothing and work. All who guide politics and economics must, in honor, make every effort to see that this aim is realized.

* * *

Extolling work in an address to three labor associations in Rome, October 19, 1963:

It is necessary to love work. The desire to work in order to earn one's daily bread is legitimate and I would say sacred.

* * *

Giving his views on the church and the artist, in a homily after an artists' mass in the Sistine Chapel, May 7, 1964:

We have always been friends. But as happens among relatives and friends, we have spoiled it a little. We have not broken, but we have disturbed our relationship. . . . We have put on a cloak of lead; forgive us!

* * *

Warning on possible perils of a cloistered life, in a speech to a gathering of nuns at Castel Gandolfo, September 8, 1964:

* * *

> *It sometimes happens that this "sense of the church" may be less wise and less cultivated in certain religious families by the fact that they live in seclusion and find in the limits of their community all the objects of immediate interest, and few know what is happening outside the enclosure of their occupation. . . .*

* * *

Commenting on the role of journalists, at a special audience for the Overseas Press Club of America, May 22, 1964:

> *Yours is the task of presenting the world as a perfect mirror without adding or subtracting to the image.*

* * *

Expressing universal love in an address to the crowds at St. Peter's Square awaiting the Pope's return from Bombay, December 5, 1964:

> *We love all men because they are all sons of God, and you must do likewise.*

* * *

Meeting with American Jewish leaders in Rome, May 30, 1964:

> *While we again strongly deplore the horrible ordeals of which the Jews have been the victims in recent years, we wish you every favor from God, whom we invoke with all our heart on your behalf, and that of all those who are near and dear to you.*

* * *

Announcing at a mass at St. Peter's on October 18, 1964, that he intended to travel to Bombay to attend the World Eucharistic Congress:

> *Yes, the Pope is becoming a missionary, which means a witness, a shepherd, an apostle on the move.*

* * *

Further outlining the purpose of his trip, in a speech at the Bombay airport, December 2, 1964:

> *We come as a pilgrim, a pilgrim of peace, of joy, of serenity and love. We greet all the Indian people—every man, woman and child, and we extend our greeting to all the nations of Asia, to every nation in the world. May they always remember that all men are brothers under the*

fatherhood of the Divinity, may they learn to love one another, to avoid violating the natural rights of others, may they ever strive to respect these rights in truth, in justice and in love.

* * *

Later, giving his reasons for visiting the Holy Land, he told Jordan's King Hussein, upon arrival in Amman, January 4, 1965:

Our visit is a spiritual one. A humble pilgrimage to the sacred places made holy by the Birth, the Life, the Passion and the Death of Jesus Christ, and by his glorious Resurrection and Ascension. At each of these venerable shrines, we shall pray for that peace which Jesus left . . . which comes from the fulfillment of his commandment: "To love one another as He loved us."

* * *

During the four-day space flight of Major James A. McDivitt and Major Edward H. White II, he told the crowds at St. Peter's Square on June 6, 1965:

Our benediction goes to all on earth and rises also to the skies for those who are exploring astral paths.

* * *

Marking the twentieth anniversary of the dropping of an atomic bomb on Hiroshima, in a speech at Castel Gandolfo, August 8, 1965:

We pray that that homicidal weapon may not have killed peace in the world; may not have injured forever the honor of science, and that it has not extinguished the serenity of life on this earth.

* * *

Commenting on papal supremacy, in his first encyclical, August 10, 1964:

It distresses us to see how we . . . are regarded by many of the separated brethren as being its [Christian unity's] stumbling block. . . . Without the Pope, the Catholic Church would no longer be Catholic.

* * *

Extolling the value of sports in a speech to the Italian Sports Association, March 20, 1965:

The spiritual elevation of persons through sports is an indispensable condition for an orderly service and constructive society.

* * *

*Following are the complete texts of the
eight statements made by Pope Paul VI
during the historic visit.*

At Rome Airport

*Statement by the Pope upon his departure from Fiumicino
Airport in Rome, translated from the Italian version released
by the Vatican press office and relayed by The Associated Press:*

In the act of undertaking our trip to United Nations headquarters, on the twentieth anniversary of the foundation of
that international organization, while we entrust to Providence
the outcome of our mission of peace and of goodwill, we send
an open, frank salutation of good wishes to all the peoples of
the world.

We know that they look upon this initiative with hope, and
we have had in the past few days numerous and very pleasing
evidence of this: with all our heart we thank them together
with their leaders. We will meet with the expert and esteemed
representatives of the individual states, assembled for constructive dialogue in the setting of United Nations headquarters.
And as we express our esteem and benevolence, it is good to
formulate this very moment an assurance and a hope.

The assurance: that our undertaking, like every word we
will utter in the coming encounters, has no other ambition, no
other purpose than to encourage, comfort and bless the forces
of men of goodwill, aimed at protecting, guaranteeing and increasing universal peace.

This is the goal that we proposed in accepting the invitation,
as courteous as it was pressing, sent us on the twentieth anniversary of the founding of the United Nations.

The hope, or better, the certainty: that our step—taken both
in sincere awareness of our limitation and with confidence in
divine help—may find a willing response in the hearts of men,
especially those who rule the destinies of peoples, just as it has
been welcomed with a unanimous and consoling response.

The world awaits and asks for peace; the world needs peace;
the world demands peace—true, stable, durable—after the sufferings of the wars which have disrupted our century, after the
immense sorrows that have devastated humanity. Mutual hos-
tilities must fall; ever-present differences must be overcome
with equable and courageous negotiations; the orderly progress

of civil life and the flowering of free activity of thought and the arts must be assured.

Only peace can guarantee this. And it is peace we ask for with a voice that has no force of arms but is invigorated by the very strength of the Prince of Peace, whose minister and representative on earth we are. We ask the heads of state as well as politicians, diplomats as well as financial and economic experts, scientists and philosophers, literary men and those of the press, for peace. All are called to lend their contribution to the great work of peace, which needs everyone in order to sink deep and ineradicable roots in our time.

With this promise and in this certitude, we start our voyage in the name of the Lord, confident, moreover, of the protection of her who is invoked as Queen of Peace. And we bless all, invoking upon each nation of the world the omnipotent protection of the Lord. Peace to you all!

Arrival at Kennedy Airport

The Pope's speech, as reported by the Papal Visit News Center:

We reply without delay to the greetings presented to us by the distinguished representatives of the United Nations, and we express our sincere thanks for the invitation extended to us to address that great Assembly. We are thus given the honor and the good fortune of meeting that greatest of all international organizations. It gives us particular pleasure to mark in this way the twentieth anniversary of the founding of the United Nations, and to express our best wishes for its permanency and its development.

Our encouragement and support have, we believe, a special meaning. This is because we come from Rome, that city which, first of all in the history of our civilization, promoted and represented the political union of peoples under the rule of law, and consequently in liberty, in culture and in peace. We come from Rome, the world city, where the *"imperium mundi,"* the empire of the world, took form and conscience. We come from Rome, where there is located the central seat of that religious society, not founded on temporal power, which is the Catholic Chuch. We are happy to note the natural sympathy existing between these two universalities, and to bear to your terrestrial city of peace the greetings and good wishes of our spiritual city of peace. One is a peace which rises from the earth, the other a peace which descends from heaven; and their meeting is most marvelous: justice and peace have kissed one another. May God grant that this be for mankind's greater good.

We also wish to reply without delay to the greetings offered us by this great country in the person of the President's representative, a country so free, so strong, so industrious, so full of wonders, this country of America, the America of the states, where we have so very many brothers, sons and friends in the faith, and where a populous nation founds its very modern civilization upon the brotherhood of its citizens.

Greetings to you, America! The first Pope to set foot upon your land blesses you with all his heart. He renews, as it were, the gesture of your discoverer, Christopher Columbus, when he planted the cross of Christ in this blessed soil. May the cross of blessing which we now trace over your skies and your land preserve those gifts which Christ gave you and guarantees to you: peace, concord, freedom, justice—and above all the vision of life in the hope of immortality. God bless this land of yours!

At St. Patrick's Cathedral

The Pope's address in English, as recorded by The New York
Times:

We thank our beloved son, Cardinal Spellman, the esteemed
Archbishop, for this warm welcome. We come to you from
Rome with the blessings of those great saints, Peter and Paul,
whose blood sanctified it, and the blessings of Christ, whose
vicar on earth we are.

To you, dear brother, pastor of this magnificent and glorious
edifice, to the bishops, clergy, religious and faithful gathered
around you, we extend the word of special greeting. Today
we feel a common citizenship with you because we are here
in your city and beautiful country. And because you are citizens
of the Church of Rome, we truly are one in sentiment. The
patron of this great cathedral, St. Patrick, once said: "As you
are Christians, so be you Romans." This we feel in a special
manner because we are all citizens of Rome.

Asking you for your prayerful support of our message for
peace we extend to all of you and to your dear ones at home,
the aged, the sick and the children in a special manner our
paternal apostolic blessing.

At the United Nations General Assembly

Translation of the Pope's address to the United Nations General Assembly, delivered in French:

As we commence our address to this unique world audience, we wish to thank your Secretary-General, U Thant, for the invitation which he extended to us to visit the United Nations, on the occasion of the twentieth anniversary of the foundation of this world institution for peace and for collaboration between the peoples of the entire earth.

Our thanks also to the President of the General Assembly, Mr. Amintore Fanfani, who used such kind language in our regard from the very day of his election.

We thank all of you here present for your kind welcome, and we extend to each one of you our deferential and sincere salutation. In friendship you have invited us and admitted us to this meeting; and it is as a friend that we are here today.

We express to you our cordial personal homage, and we bring you that of the entire Second Vatican Ecumenical Council now meeting in Rome, and represented here by the eminent cardinals who accompany us for this purpose.

In their name and in our own, to each and every one of you, honor and greeting.

This encounter, as you all understand, marks a simple and, at the same time, a great moment. It is simple because you have before you a humble man, your brother, and among you all, representatives of sovereign states, the least invested, if you wish to think of him thus, with a minuscule, as it were symbolic, temporal sovereignty, only as much as is necessary to be free to exercise his spiritual mission, and to assure all those who deal with him that he is independent of every other sovereignty of this world. But he, who now addresses you, has no temporal power, nor any ambition to compete with you. In fact, we have nothing to ask for, no question to raise. We have only a desire to express and a permission to request: namely, that of serving you insofar as we can, with disinterest, with humility and love.

This is our first declaration. As you can see, it is so simple as to seem insignificant to this assembly, which always treats of most important and most difficult matters.

We said also, however, and all here today feel it, that this moment is also a great one—great for us, great for you.

For us: you know well who we are. Whatever may be the opinion you have of the Pontiff of Rome, you know our mission. We are the bearer of a message for all mankind. And this we are, not only in our own personal name and in the name of the great Catholic family, but also in that of those Christian brethren who share the same sentiments which we express here, particularly of those who so kindly charged us explicitly to be their spokesman here. Like a messenger who, after a long journey, finally succeeds in delivering the letter which has been entrusted to him, so we appreciate the good fortune of this moment, however brief, which fulfills a desire nourished in the heart for nearly twenty centuries. For, as you will remember, we are very ancient; we here represent a long history; we here celebrate the epilogue of a wearying pilgrimage in search of a conversation with the entire world, ever since the command was given to us: Go and bring the good news to all peoples. Now, you here represent all peoples. Allow us to tell you that we have a message, a happy message, to deliver to each one of you and to all.

1. We might call our message a ratification, a solemn moral ratification of this lofty institution. This message comes from our historical experience. As "an expert in humanity," we bring to this organization the suffrage of our recent predecessors, that of the entire Catholic episcopate and our own, convinced as we are that this organization represents the obligatory path of modern civilization and of world peace. In saying this, we feel we are making our own the voice of the dead and of the living; of the dead, who fell in the terrible wars of the past; of the living who survived those wars, bearing in their hearts a condemnation of those who would try to renew wars; and also of those living who rise up fresh and confident, the youth of the present generation, who legitimately dream of a better human race.

And we also make our own the voice of the poor, the disinherited, the suffering, of those who hunger and thirst for justice, for the dignity of life, for freedom, for well-being and progress. The peoples of the earth turn to the United Nations as the last hope of concord and peace. We presume to present here, with their tribute of honor and of hope, our own tribute also. That is why this moment is great for you, also.

2. We feel that you are already aware of this. Hearken now to the continuation of our message. It becomes a message of good wishes for the future. The edifice which you have constructed must never fall; it must be perfected and made equal to the needs which world history will present. You mark a stage in the development of mankind from which retreat must never be admitted, but from which it is necessary that advance be made.

To the plurality of states, which can no longer ignore one another, you offer an extremely simple and fruitful formula of coexistence. First of all, you recognize and distinguish the one and the others. You do not confer existence upon states, but you qualify each single nation as fit to sit in the orderly congress of peoples. That is, you grant recognition, of the highest ethical and juridical value, to each single sovereign national community, guaranteeing it an honored international citizenship. This in itself is a great service to the cause of humanity, namely, to define clearly and to honor the national subjects of the world community, and to confirm them in a juridical status, worthy thereby of being recognized and respected by all, and from which there may derive an orderly and stable system of international life. You give sanction to the great principle that the relations between peoples should be regulated by reason, by justice, by law, by negotiation; not by force, nor by violence, not by war, not by fear or by deceit. Thus it must be.

Allow us to congratulate you for having had the wisdom to open this hall to the younger peoples, to those states which have recently attained independence and national freedom. Their presence is the proof of the universality and magnanimity which inspire the principles of this institution. Thus it must be. This is our praise and our good wish, and, as you can see, we do not bestow these as from outside. We derive them from inside, from the very essence of your institution.

3. Your Charter goes further than this, and our message advances with it. You exist and operate to unite the nations, to bind states together. Let us use this second formula: to bring the one together with the others. You are an association. You are a bridge between peoples. You are a network of relations between states. We would almost say that your chief characteristic is a reflection, as it were, in the temporal field, of what our Catholic Church aspires to be in the spiritual field: unique and universal. In the ideological construction of mankind, there is on the natural level nothing superior to this. Your vocation is to make brothers not only of some, but of all peoples. A difficult undertaking, indeed; but this it is, your most noble undertaking. Is there anyone who does not see the necessity of coming thus progressively to the establishment of a world authority, able to act efficaciously on the juridical and political levels?

Once more we reiterate our good wish: go forward always. We will go further, and say: Strive to bring back among you any who have separated themselves, and study the right method of uniting to your pact of brotherhood, in honor and loyalty, those who do not yet share in it. Act so that those still outside will desire and merit the confidence of all, and then be generous in granting such confidence. You have the good fortune and the honor of sitting in this assembly of peaceful nations. Hear us as we say: see to it that the reciprocal trust which here unites you, and enables you to do good and great things, may never be undermined or betrayed.

4. The inherent logic of this wish, which might be considered to pertain to the very structure of your organization, leads us to complete it with other formulas. Thus, let no one, inasmuch as he is a member of your union, be superior to the others: Never one above the other. This is the formula of equality. We are well aware that it must be completed by the evaluation of other factors besides simple membership in this institution; but equality, too, belongs to its constitution. You are not equal, but here you make yourselves equal. For several among you, this may be an act of high virtue; allow us to say this to you, as the representative of a religion which accomplishes salvation through the humility of its divine Founder. Men cannot be brothers if they are not humble. It is pride, no matter how legitimate it may seem to be, which provokes tension and struggles for prestige, for predominance, colonialism, egoism; that is, pride disrupts brotherhood.

5. And now our message reaches its highest point, which is, at first, a negative point. You are expecting us to utter this sentence, and we are well aware of its gravity and solemnity: Not the ones against the others, never again, never more. It was principally for this purpose that the organization of the United Nations arose: against war, in favor of peace. Listen to the lucid words of the great departed John Kennedy, who proclaimed four years ago: "Mankind must put an end to war, or war will put an end to mankind."

Many words are not needed to proclaim this loftiest aim of your institution. It suffices to remember that the blood of millions of men, that numberless and unheard-of sufferings, useless slaughter and frightful ruin, are the sanction of the pact which unites you, with an oath which must change the future history of the world: No more war, war never again! Peace, it is peace which must guide the destinies of peoples and of all mankind. We have even suffered the loss of great men in this sacred cause.

Gratitude to you, glory to you, who for twenty years have labored for peace. Gratitude and glory to you for the conflicts which have prevented or have brought to an end. The results of your efforts in recent days in favor of peace, even if not yet proved decisive, are such as to deserve that we, presuming to interpret the sentiments of the whole world, express to you both praise and thanks.

Gentlemen, you have performed and you continue to perform a great work: the education of mankind in the ways of peace. The United Nations is the great school where that education is imparted, and we are today in the assembly hall of that school. Everyone taking his place here becomes a pupil and also a teacher in the art of building peace. When you leave this hall, the world looks upon you as the architects and constructors of peace.

Peace, as you know, is not built up only by means of politics, by the balance of forces and of interests. It is constructed with the mind, with ideas, with works of peace. You labor in this great construction. But you are still at the beginning of your task. Will the world ever succeed in changing that selfish and bellicose mentality which, up to now, has been interwoven with so much of its history? It is hard to foresee. But it is easy to affirm that it is toward that new history, a peaceful, truly human, history, as promised by God to men of goodwill, that we must resolutely march. The roads thereto are already well marked out for you; and the first is that of disarmament.

If you wish to be brothers, let the arms fall from your hands. One cannot love while holding offensive arms. Those armaments, especially those terrible arms which modern science has given you, long before they produce victims and ruins, nourish bad feelings, create nightmares, distrust and somber resolves; they demand enormous expenditures; they obstruct projects of union and useful collaboration; they falsify the very psychology of peoples. As long as man remains that weak, changeable and even wicked being that he often shows himself to be, defensive arms will, unfortunately, be necessary. You, however, in your courage and valor, are studying the ways of guaranteeing the security of international life, without having recourse to arms. This is a most noble aim, this the peoples expect of you, this must be achieved.

Let unanimous trust in this institution grow, let its authority increase, and this aim, we believe, will be secured. Gratitude will be expressed to you by all peoples, relieved as they will then be from the crushing expenses of armaments and freed from the nightmare of an ever-imminent war.

We rejoice in the knowledge that many of you have considered favorably our invitation, addressed to all states in the cause of peace from Bombay last December, to divert to the benefit of the developing countries at least a part of the savings which could be realized by reducing armaments. We here renew that invitation, trusting in your sentiments of humanity and generosity.

6. In so doing, we become aware that we are echoing another principle which is fundamental to the United Nations, which is its positive and affirmative high point; namely, that you work here not only to avert conflicts between states, but also to make them capable of working for each other. You are not satisfied with facilitating mere coexistence between nations; you take a much greater step forward, one deserving of our praise and our support: you organize the brotherly collabora-

tion of peoples. In this way a system of solidarity is set up, and its lofty civilized aims win the orderly and unanimous support of all the family of peoples for the common good and for the good of each individual. This aspect of the organization of the United Nations is the most beautiful; it is its most truly human aspect; it is the ideal of which mankind dreams on its pilgrimage through time; it is the world's greatest hope; it is, we presume to say, the reflection of the loving and transcendent design of God for the progress of the human family on earth—a reflection in which we see the message of the Gospel, which is heavenly become earthly. Indeed, it seems to us that here we hear the echo of the voice of our predecessors, and particularly of Pope John XXIII, whose message of "Pacem in Terris" was so honorably and significantly received among you.

You proclaim here the fundamental rights and duties of man, his dignity, his freedom—and, above all, his religious freedom. We feel that you thus interpret the highest sphere of human wisdom and, we might add, its sacred character. For you deal here above all with human life. And the life of man is sacred; no one may dare offend it. Respect for life, even with regard to the great problem of the birth rate must find here in your assembly its highest affirmation and its most reasoned defense. You must strive to multiply bread so that it suffices for the tables of mankind, and not rather favor an artificial control of birth, which would be irrational, in order to diminish the number of guests at the banquet of life.

It does not suffice, however, to feed the hungry; it is necessary also to assure to each man a life conformed to his dignity. This, too, you strive to perform. We may consider this the fulfillment before our very eyes, and by your efforts, of that prophetical announcement so applicable to your institution: "They will melt down their swords into plowshares, [and] their spears into pruning hooks." Are you not using the prodigious energies of the earth and the magnificent inventions of science, no longer as instruments of death but as tools of life for humanity's new era?

We know how intensive and ever more effective are the efforts of the United Nations and its dependent world agencies to assist those governments who need help to hasten their economic and social progress.

We know how ardently you labor to overcome illiteracy and to spread good culture throughout the world; to give men adequate modern medical assistance; to employ in man's service the marvelous resources of science, of technology and of organization—all of this is magnificent, and merits the praise and support of all, including our own.

We ourself wish to give the good example, even though the smallness of our means is inadequate to the practical and quantitative needs. We intend to intensify the development of our charitable institutions to combat world hunger and to meet world needs. It is thus, and in no other way, that peace can be built up.

7. One more word, gentlemen, our final word: this edifice which you are constructing does not rest upon merely material and earthly foundations, for thus it would be a house built upon sand; above all, it is based on our own consciences. The hour has struck for our "conversion," for personal transformation, for interior renewal. We must get used to thinking of man in a new way; and in a new way also of men's life in common; with a new manner, too, of conceiving the paths of history and the destiny of the world, according to the words of St. Paul: "You must be clothed in the new self, which is created in God's image, justified and sanctified through the truth."

The hour has struck for a halt, a moment of recollection, of reflection, almost of prayer. A moment to think anew of our common origin, our history, our common destiny. Today as never before, in our era so marked by human progress, there is need for an appeal to the moral conscience of man. For the danger comes, not from progress, nor from science—indeed, if properly utilized, these could rather resolve many of the grave problems which assail mankind. No, the real danger comes from man himself, wielding ever more powerful instruments which can be employed equally well for destruction or for the loftiest conquests.

In a word, then, the edifice of modern civilization must be built upon spiritual principles which alone can, not only support it, but even illuminate and animate it. We believe, as you know, that these indispensable principles of superior wisdom must be founded upon faith in God, that unknown God of whom St. Paul spoke to the Athenians in the Areopagus; unknown to them, although without realizing it, they sought Him and He was close to them, as happens also to many men of our times. To us, in any case, and to all those who accept the ineffable revelation which Christ has given us of Him, He is the living God, the Father of all men.

At Holy Family Church

The Pope delivered this statement in English:

It is indeed a distinct pleasure for us to have this opportunity, however brief, during our visit to the United Nations to greet you, one and all, representatives of the various organizations maintaining relations with the United Nations.

We express our cordial good wishes to the members of the many Catholic organizations who collaborate with the United Nations to bring the benefits of this international organization to all parts of the world. We derive satisfaction also from the fact that our own observers, at least some, are among you, and we wish to make specific mention of Monsignor Alberto Giovannetti, who has the responsible position of Permanent Observer of the Holy See to the United Nations.

In a way, we have left our purely spiritual sphere of activity in order to know your work for peace, to which you are dedicating yourselves so earnestly, and to collaborate with you insofar as it is possible for us, and to associate ourselves in a certain measure with your efforts.

We have said in our discourse that peace is the work not only of political wisdom; it is not a result brought about only by pacts or treaties. Rather it is necessary to favor, encourage, establish and assure peace continually with concrete and specialized organs of peace—and these you are.

We, therefore, have great admiration for you and for your dedicated labors. You are worthy of honor and your efforts merit the grateful prayers of all mankind. We urge you with our heart to work even more strenuously for the cause of peace—a peace based on the fatherhood of God and the brotherhood of all men. This is the message of our Divine Saviour, the Prince of Peace; this is the message we wish to leave you today.

This message we intend not only for the Catholic organizations represented at the United Nations; but we likewise extend it to all of you present, representing various Protestant and Jewish organizations accredited with the various organizations of the United Nations. The work of peace is not restricted to one religious belief, it is the work and duty of every human person, regardless of his religious conviction. Men are brothers, God is their father, and their Father wills that they live in peace with one another as brothers should.

For our part, we thank you for the cordial friendship which you have accorded our observers and we promise our collaboration insofar as we can join in your studies, your programs and activities, and to this we join our prayers for the success of your efforts and for God's choicest blessings on your noble endeavors.

At Yankee Stadium

The Pope delivered this homily in English:

Brothers and sons of New York,
Brothers and sons of the United States and of all America.
All of you who have assembled here from every part of the world,
We greet you and we bless you!

This is the day which the Lord has made; let us rejoice and be glad today! This is the day which we have desired for centuries! The day which, for the first time, sees the Pope setting foot on this young and glorious continent! A historic day, for it recalls and crowns the long years of the evangelization of America, and the magnificent development of the church in the United States! All honor to you, brothers and sons! Peace and joy in Christ to you, whom we wish we could individually receive and embrace! A fraternal and brotherly greeting to you, bishops and pastors, to you, priests, men and women religious of America! To the shepherd of this most flourishing archdiocese, Francis Cardinal Spellman, Archbishop of New York, who is here beside us, our greeting and blessing, as a token of our veneration and our affection, of our gratitude to him and our esteem; especially today, on the feast of St. Francis of Assisi, our best wishes on his name day; and together with him we greet and salute the entire Catholic community of New York and of all the United States of America. We know your pastoral work and your faithfulness; we know the splendid organization and spiritual vitality of your parishes, of your seminaries, of your universities, of your schools, of your hospitals, of your works of charity! We know too your love for Christ and His church. We affirm to you what St. Paul wrote to the Romans: "Your faith is proclaimed all over the world" (Romans 1:8). And it is from Rome that we bring you that message of faith and love which unites us all in Christ; together with the blessing of Sts. Peter and Paul.

We are most happy to greet at the same time, with all reverence and sincerity, those Christian brothers here present, separated from us, yet united with us by baptism and by belief in the Lord Jesus. We keep them all in our heart and in our prayers. We also greet those here present who follow other religious beliefs, and who in good conscience intend to seek and honor Almighty God, the Lord of heaven and earth; among whom the descendants of Abraham have our particular consideration.

We feel, too, that the entire American people is here present, with its noblest and most characteristic traits: a people basing its conception of life on spiritual values, on a religious sense, on freedom, on loyalty, on work, on the respect of duty, on family affection, on generosity and courage. We pay honor to the human and civil virtues of this great people, and in these virtues we recognize valuable derivations from Christian values, which we hope will ever remain living and active, safeguarding the American spirit from those dangers which prosperity itself can entail, and which the materialism of our day can make even more menacing. From its brief but heroic history, this young and flourishing country can derive lofty and convincing examples to encourage it in its future progress.

So, too, we turn our thoughts cordially to all those who belong to other nations and are present at this great religious assembly; they show forth the hospitality of this country, and also the fact that men of different origins can live together, work together and prosper together in freedom and in concord. To all of them and to their respective countries we send our greetings and good wishes.

What are we to say to you, that can correspond to the duties of our apostolic ministry and be adequate to the spirit of this unique occasion? Our words can only be the words of the Gospel, which has just been read to you; the words of the risen Jesus, which He repeated three times: Peace be to you!

Truly, verily, peace be to you!

How rich in meaning, how abundant in good things, is this divine and human greeting of peace! Repeated thousands of times, we all recognize it, we all desire it. And that is good. But allow us to exhort you to consider it once again, to preserve it as the Gospel message of the Pope as he lands on this soil and proclaims to all those he meets: Peace be to this house, to this continent, and to all those who inhabit it!

We have, then, three things to say to you.

First of all, you must love peace. Here we can use the words of Christ: "Blessed are the peacemakers, for they shall be called the sons of God" (Matthew 5:9). If we truly wish to be Christians, we must love peace, we must make our own the cause of peace, we must meditate on the real meaning of peace, we must conform our minds to the thought of peace. In the past, it was not always so in the education of minds and the training of citizens; but today it must be so; we must love peace, because its dwelling is first in men's hearts, and only afterward in the external condition of society. Peace must live and reign in men's consciences, as Holy Scripture teaches us: "May the peace of Christ reign in your hearts" (Colossians 3:15). Peace is order, in relation to God and in relation to men; it is wisdom, it is justice, it is civilization. Whoever loves peace loves mankind, without distinction of race or color.

Second thought: You must serve the cause of peace. Serve it, and not make use of it for aims other than the true aims of peace. Serve it, and not use this noble standard as a cover for cowardice or selfishness, which refuses to make sacrifices for the common good; nor debilitate and pervert the spirit, by evading the call of duty and seeking one's own interests and pleasure. Peace is not a state which can be acquired and made permanent. Peace must be built; it must be built up every day by works of peace. These works of peace are, first of all, social order; then, aid to the poor, who still make up an immense multitude of the world population, aid to the needy, the weak, the sick, the ignorant. Peace must be like a garden, in which public and private beneficence cultivates the choicest flowers of friendship, of solidarity, of charity and love.

Third thought: Peace must be based on moral and religious principles, which will make it sincere and stable. Politics do not suffice to sustain a durable peace. The absence of conflict does not suffice to make of peace a source of happiness and of true human progress. Peace must have its roots anchored in wisdom, and this wisdom must draw nourishment from the true concept of life, that is, the Christian concept. Remember the words of the Lord Jesus: "Peace I leave with you, *My* peace I give to you. Not as the world gives do I give to you" (John 14:27). Jesus, the Prince of Peace (Isaiah 9:6), has His own original and characteristic peace, which can regulate every human relationship because, in the very first place, it regulates the relationship with God.

Coming among you at a moment, so beautiful, so brief but so important, as this, we have no better greeting, no better remembrance for you than to repeat that holy salutation of Christ: Peace, His peace!

Finally, one more word.

At the end of this mass, we shall bless a stone, which we had removed from St. Peter's Basilica and which we ourself brought here from Rome. This blessed stone will be placed in the foundations of a great new edifice, the Seminary of the Archdiocese of New York. Cardinal Spellman, with the courage and farsightedness which are characteristic of him, is preparing to build this seminary for the new and future generations of students for the priesthood in the service of the Holy Mother Church. This is indeed a monument worthy of perpetuating the memory of our visit to you. You can see in this cornerstone an eloquent symbol of the faith and love which unite the Catholics of New York to the Church of Rome. You can see in this ceremony the proof of our confidence in the seminarians of New York, those of today and those of tomorrow; the pledge of our good wishes that they may always be sustained by Christ, and always be the *gloria Christi,* the glory of Christ (II Corinthians 8:23). God bless you.

At the World's Fair

A statement released by papal representatives, but not read by the Pontiff, during his visit to the Vatican Pavilion at the World's Fair:

We have to come to see the beautiful setting for the masterpiece of Michelangelo, the Pietà. It is easy to understand how so many millions of visitors have been attracted by this precious sculpture intended to honor the Blessed Lady and her crucified Son. We are confident that it has moved countless souls and has given inspiration to artists to imitate the genius of this great artist.

We congratulate our brother, Cardinal Spellman, and all those who have collaborated to produce this wonderful and prayerful result. No expense and sacrifice has been spared to prepare a setting worthy for such a subject.

We have offered our prayers to Christ, the Good Shepherd, whose message of peace and concord we have come to proclaim, and we are confident that through the intercession of our Blessed Lady our prayers will bear fruit.

As we gazed on this moving masterpiece, we could not but think of the religious convictions which moved the young Michelangelo to such heights and to such a magnificent result. We feel that these same religious convictions can move men in a similar way to seek peace and harmony among the peoples of this world.

We bless all of you invoking upon you an abundance of heavenly blessings and graces.

Statement to the Press

The Pope's statement was released at his departure from Kennedy Airport. He did not deliver these remarks in person:

Gentlemen of the press, radio, television and cinema:
Our crowded schedule did not permit us the time to meet with you, but we cannot depart without expressing a word of admiration and respect for your profession and vocation. Communications have experienced a remarkable advance since our first contact many years ago. As a result the world has become much smaller. Behind each one of you is a vast network working to bring the latest news to everyone. Responsibility is in proportion to knowledge and you are in possession of much weighty knowledge. You can lead men to be aware of the complex problems and you can encourage them to make their own personal contribution without which true peace and harmony cannot ever become a reality.

Your labors are often hidden and go unheralded, but be sure that we appreciate them and value them highly. We are confident that you will not falter in bringing the message of peace to all men of goodwill, that you will continue to teach men that all are brothers of one human family, and that you will help them understand one another and to cooperate in an atmosphere of mutual respect and affection. Our good wishes and our heartfelt thanks go to you for your most important work. May God bless you!

Departure from Kennedy Airport

The text of the Pope's speech at Kennedy International Airport before departing on the return flight to Rome:

We are sincerely grateful to you all, for the greetings which you express to us by your presence here.

We thank the President, the Secretary-General and all the members of the United Nations; the President of the United States of America and the federal authorities; the Governor of the State of New York and the state officials; the Mayor of the City of New York and municipal officials. Our gratitude goes also to the Cardinal Archbishop of the city, and to the priests, the religious leaders and faithful people. And we are grateful to all the citizens of this great metropolis and of all the United States of America, for their enthusiastic and affectionate welcome.

Our very brief visit has given us a great honor: that of proclaiming to the whole world, from the headquarters of the United Nations, Peace! We shall never forget this extraordinary hour. Nor can we bring it to a more fitting conclusion than by expressing the wish that this central seat of human relationships for the civil peace of the world may ever be conscious and worthy of its high privilege.

To America, our prayerful wishes for prosperity and peace, under the rule of law, in concord with the other nations of the world; and our heartfelt blessings upon its people, their families, their government, their homes and schools and churches, one nation, under God, free and indivisible. God bless America! God bless you all!